My Voice

Danny Herman

Manchester University Press

Danny Herman

Run Danny Run

Manchester University Press

Copyright © The Fed 2022, 2024

The Fed (being the trading name of The Federation of Jewish Services) is the proprietor or licensee ('rightsholder') of all intellectual property rights in relation to this work including but not limited to copyright, content and images. No part of this work may be translated, reprinted, transmitted, reproduced or utilised without prior permission in writing from The Fed and Manchester University Press, except in accordance with permitted uses and provisions of the Copyright, Designs and Patents Act 1988. Regarding images included herein, unless otherwise indicated, all rights are reserved and permission to use figures must be obtained from the rightsholder.

The Fed has asserted its moral rights as the author of this work. The My Voice collection has been produced using the original recordings of conversations between Fed clients and Fed volunteer befrienders. The My Voice Project is committed to ensuring the work depicts actual life events in survivor's words, which are as truthful as recollection permits and/or can be verified by research.

Every effort has been made to contact the copyright owners for the images used in this book. If you have any queries, please contact the publisher.

British Library Cataloguing-in-Publication Data
A catalogue record for this book is available from the British Library

Published by Manchester University Press
Oxford Road, Manchester M13 9PL

www.manchesteruniversitypress.co.uk

ISBN 978 1 5261 8628 7   paperback

First published by The Fed in 2022
This edition first published by Manchester University Press in 2024

Typeset by Lumina Datamatics

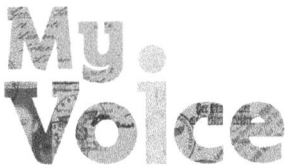

The Fed's My Voice Project documents and publishes the life stories of Holocaust survivors and refugees living in Greater Manchester, the North West and London. The oral history, which is recorded and transcribed, captures their entire lives from before, during and after the war years. The books are written in the words of the survivor so that future generations can always hear their voice. The My Voice book collection is a valuable resource for Holocaust awareness and education and is housed in many prestigious institutions and libraries around the world.

Danny Herman shared his journey and experiences with Fed volunteer Sharon Inerfield, who visited him during 2019 and 2021.

These are Danny's words.

This is his story.

Dedicated to:

My parents

Gretchen 24.07.1910 – 07.05.2007

Siegie 30.10.1904 – 15.02.1979

"I do not bring forgiveness with me, nor forgetfulness. The only ones who can forgive are dead; the living have no right to forget."

Chaim Herzog

In loving memory of the members of the Herrmann families who perished at the hands of the Nazis during the Holocaust

All those listed were born and lived in or near Königsberg, East Prussia (now Kaliningrad, Russia).

My grandparents Hugo and Clara Herrmann
Hugo was born in 1868. Clara was born in 1877.
Both perished in 1943 in Sobibor Concentration Camp.

My paternal aunt Margarete and uncle Leo Ledermann
Leo was born in 1898. Margarete was born in 1903.
Both perished in 1942.

My first cousin Gerhard Ledermann
Gerhard was born in 1928.
He perished in 1942.

Other relatives who perished

Grete Jaruslawsky
Born in 1873. Perished in 1942.

Elli Lowenberg

Willi Lowenberg

Lotte Jaruslawsky
Born in 1903. Perished in 1938.

Moritz Polnow
Born in 1902. Perished in 1940.

Irwin Petzal

Alfred Petzal

Hans Herrmann
Born in 1892. Perished in 1942.

Heinz Herrmann

Bianca Herrmann

Also missing and presumed dead

The Rosemann family
Moritz Drewienka
Irma Schlichowsky
Simion Schlichowsky

Contents

Family tree: Herrmann branch   xiii

1. My early years in Königsberg   2
2. How my parents met and married   13
3. My father's escape to the Kitchener Camp   28
4. My father's letters to Walter   43
5. My arrival in England   48
6. My foster family   56
7. Moving to Mabfield Road   64
8. My father's internment   71
9. Life in Liverpool during the war   77
10. Moving to Manchester   82
11. The fate of those left behind   86
12. School and my Bar Mitzvahs   100
13. Changing names and naturalisation   114
14. Meeting Pat   120
15. University and a passion for athletics   129
16. The 1957 Maccabiah Games   135
17. A traditional proposal   142
18. Married life   150

Contents

19	My business ventures	156
20	Winning a gold medal at the 1961 Maccabiah Games	160
21	Our children	167
22	Finding time for my athletic activities	176
23	The European Maccabi Games	183
24	My involvement with Manchester City	185
25	Memories of the children growing up with my parents	193
26	My veteran athletic career and The Foxtrotters	198
27	Our children's career paths, grandchildren and great grandchildren	206
28	Our holidays	220
29	My volunteering roles	230
30	Returning to Vienna and Holland	236
31	Our famous seder plate	238
32	My sporting life reflections	241
33	My thoughts on antisemitism and my involvement in Holocaust education	243
34	Ellen Rawson	246
35	We have to remember	250
36	My sporting achievements timeline	253
Glossary		256
My Voice volunteers		259
About The Fed		260

Family tree: Herrmann branch

Hugo Herrmann = Clara
1868 - 1943   1877 - 1943

Margarete Herrmann
1903 - 1942
=
Leo Ledermann
1898 - 1942

Gerhard Ledermann
1928 - 1942

Siegfried Herrmann
1904 - 1979
=
Margarete Maria Eva Schultz
1910 - 2007

Daniel = Patricia Benster
b. 1935   b. 1938

Linda Claire
b. 1963
=
Barry Mark Price
b. 1960

Karen Jacqueline
b. 1964
=
Robert Duncan Wright
b. 1953

Keith Hugo
b. 1967
=
1. Lesley Finkel
   b. 1963
2. Sara Cohen
   b. 1970

Julie Vanessa
b. 1971
=
Damian Stuart Besbrode
b. 1971

My children, grandchildren and great-grandchildren

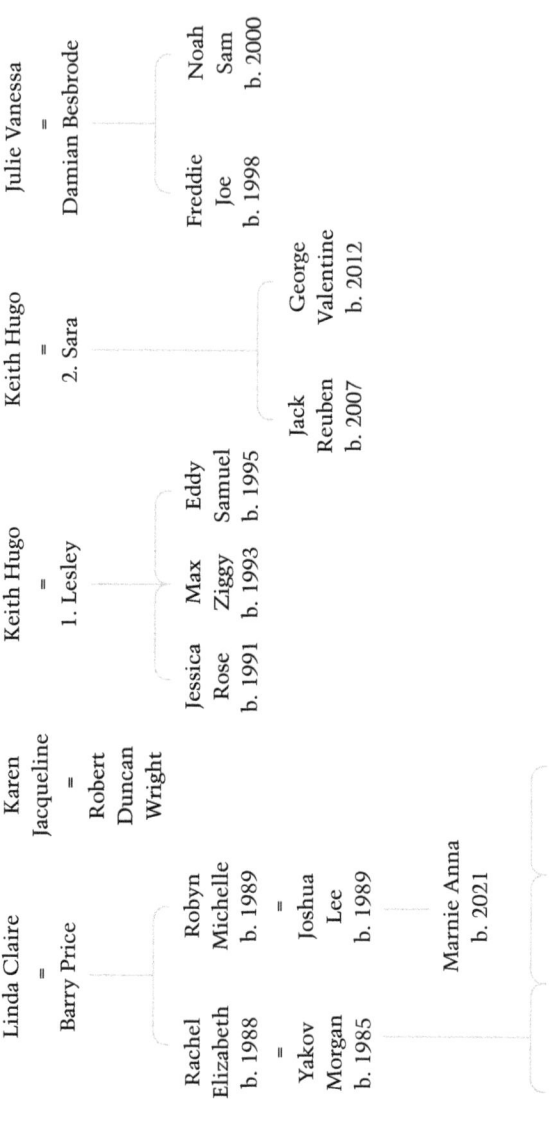

A note by Danny's eldest daughter, Linda Price

Run Danny Run

"Danny ran with his parents, fleeing Nazi Germany in 1939, the same moment the song 'Run, Rabbit, Run' was produced in England.

Danny continued to run around from toddler to teenager. His parents ran around him, nurturing and protecting Danny, the centre of their world.

His love for running started at school and continues to this day as a central theme to his and all our lives."

Chapter 1

My early years in Königsberg

I was born Daniel Herrmann on 15 September 1935 in Königsberg in East Prussia. At the end of the First World War, East Prussia was separated from mainland Germany by the so called 'Polish Corridor', as you had to go through Poland to get there. At the end of the Second World War, Königsberg was annexed by Russia and renamed Kaliningrad. If you watch football, England played against Belgium in the qualifying rounds in Kaliningrad in the 2018 World Cup in Russia. However, I think it is now unrecognisable when compared to Königsberg in 1935.

I have never been back since I left, but some of my Israeli relatives visited Kaliningrad a few years back and told me there were only about five buildings still standing that they recognised. It had been completely obliterated, if not by the Russians, then by the British bombing it in the Second World War.

If you ask me if I can remember anything of Königsberg, the answer is sadly no, very little. I was just short of my fourth birthday when I left, and I can remember only two or three things vaguely. However,

I'm not sure whether I really remember or whether my parents told me about them.

The Herrmann family seems to go back to 1760. My paternal grandparents, Clara and Hugo Herrmann, lived at 13a Claarstrasse, Königsberg. My grandfather Hugo was born in 1868 and his wife, Clara, in 1877. Hugo had a few brothers and one of them emigrated to Israel in around 1935. They were all Zionists. My grandparents had a holiday home on the coast, about 10 miles outside of Königsberg, in a place called Rauschen, which is very famous for the semi-precious stone amber. It has some nice woodlands, forests and parkland. I vaguely remember going for a walk in this bit of parkland and being pulled along by my grandfather whilst I was sitting in a small truck, like a farm vehicle with steep sides made from spindles. It's a very vague memory.

I have plenty of photographs of my paternal grandparents, Clara and Hugo, but I haven't got many of my maternal ones, Ludwig and Marie. I have discovered from later correspondence that my maternal grandparents didn't get on well and eventually divorced.

I have one other memory, which is of my maternal grandfather who was a cobbler. He specialised in anything to do with horses, so he made riding boots and all that sort of stuff. I do remember he had some sort of wood workshop, which was somewhere in Königsberg. I don't know whether other people can remember what they did when they were three or four, but those are the only two memories I have.

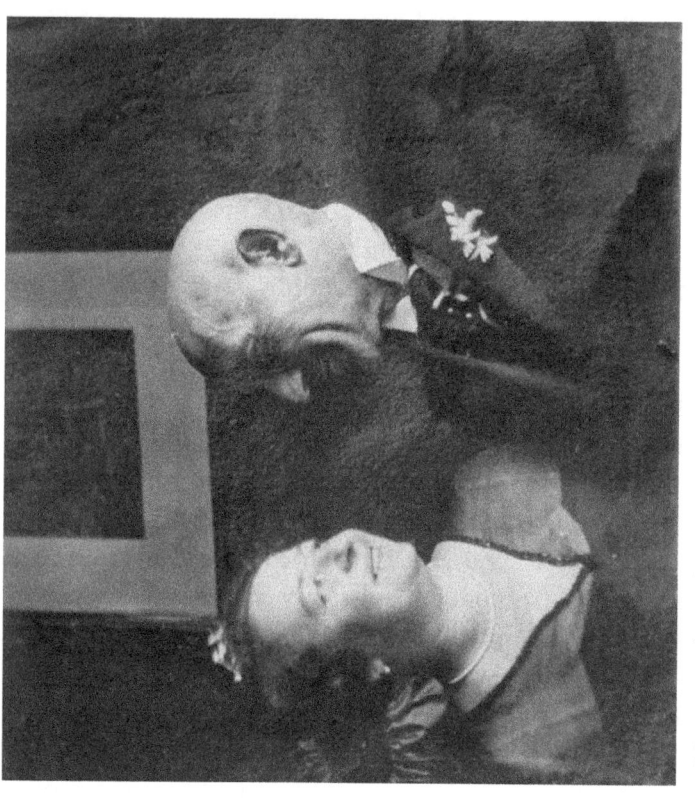

1 My paternal grandparents Clara and Hugo Herrmann on their silver wedding anniverary, 17 May 1925

My early years in Königsberg

I am an only child. People often used to ask my mother why she didn't have more children. She would explain that times were so uncertain then, and they didn't know what was going to happen. I can't remember anything about what home was like back then. I have an address for our flat and a picture of me outside the block of flats.

2 My mother holding me in the maternity hospital, September 1935

3 Me outside our block of flats in Königsberg, aged two, circa 1937

My early years in Königsberg

4 Me aged two on a shopping trip in Königsberg, 1937

5 Me sitting on some rocks, the day after my third birthday, 16 September 1938

My early years in Königsberg

6 Me with my mother and father, 1936

7 Me in the pram on the left aged one, 22 November 1936

8 Me, almost two years old, June 1937

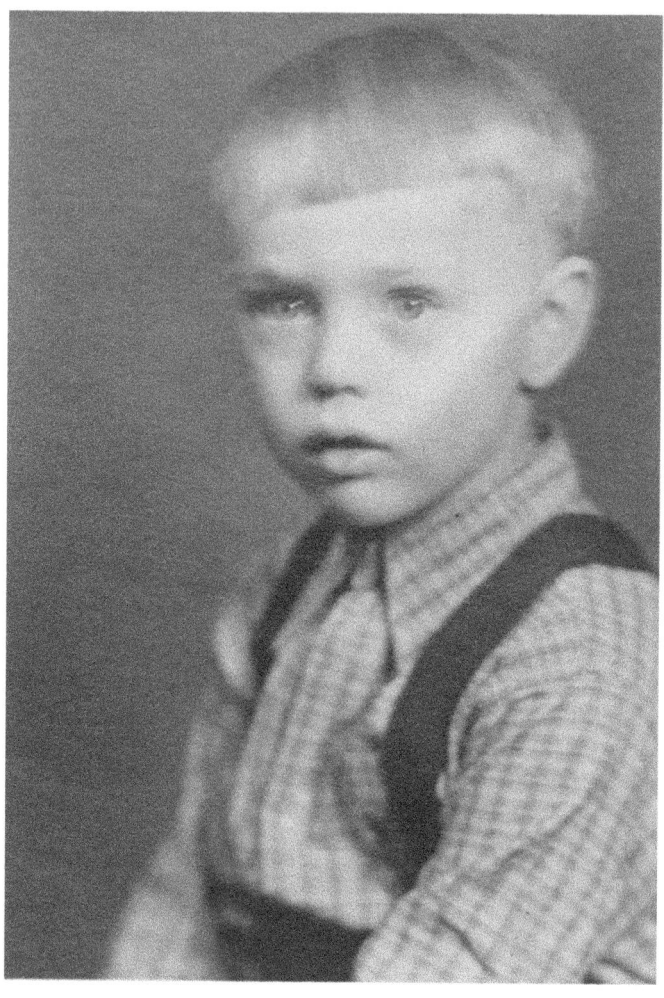

9 Me aged three

Chapter 2

How my parents met and married

My father, Siegfried Herrmann, was known as Siegie, and he was born in 1904. He had a sister called Margarete or Gretchen, which is the diminutive form. After leaving school, he went to college and studied textile engineering, which came in very useful later. He belonged to a rowing club in Königsberg, and I think he was what we call a 'cox'. I don't know what they called the club, but I'm guessing it was the Maccabi Jewish Rowing Club.

My father was in partnership with his father, Hugo, in a wholesale hosiery business called Siegfried and Hugo Herrmann. I couldn't understand why the firm was called Siegfried and Hugo Herrmann with my father's name appearing first. It was only recently that I understood why this was. Let me explain.

My father had a second cousin known as 'old Hans Sturmann' who emigrated to Israel before the war. He was a bit older than my father and part of the Herrmann family. He retired to an old people's home, and he decided to write a book about the Herrmann and the Sturmann families. It started in the year 1760 and went up to around 1971, consisting of small cameos about many members of the family.

Hans gave a handwritten copy of the book to my father and when my father died in February 1979, I decided to translate it. However, it is 125 pages long and I only recently finished it! It is written in very flowery, old-fashioned and descriptive German, so I had to use a dictionary and sometimes a German-speaking friend, Benny Brettler, to help me with it.

After I had finished translating this book, I realised that the 'Siegfried' in the name of my father's firm did not refer to my father, but to his late uncle who had started the business together with Grandfather Hugo many years earlier. He had died in 1900, before my father was born. It worked out quite well as, when my father was old enough to join the firm as a partner at the age of around 28, there was no need to change the name! I imagine that my father was named after his uncle.

My mother's name was Margarete, also Gretchen for short. She was born in 1910 and her maiden name was Schultz. Her younger brother was called Walter, and his wife was also called Margarete or Gretchen. It seemed as if all the women in Germany were called Gretchen! My mother's older brother was called Fritz.

My mother worked as a secretary for Steinberg's cigar importers and met my father at the firm's Christmas party. I am not sure why my father was invited as well, but they got to know each other. It would have been around 1929.

10 My father, aged seven with his sister Gretchen, aged nine, 1911

11 My father's *Bar Mitzvah*
My father with his mother Clara and sister Gretchen, October 1917

12 My father (wearing glasses) and three friends on the beach at Rauschen, the seaside resort near Königsberg, circa 1924

13 My father's rowing club, Königsberg.
My father is sitting down holding the flags, circa 1925.

14 My father's sister Gretchen (sitting centrally) at her engagement to Leo Ledermann, circa 1926.
My father is standing on the far left.

15 My father on one of his business trips, 22 March 1929

How my parents met and married

16 My father, 1932

When they were first 'walking out', courting the old-fashioned way, my mother always used to tell the story of how they first arranged a date. Apparently, my father was half an hour late and my mother was very annoyed. She said to him, "If you ever do that again, I'm not going out with you anymore." So he was really worried and he didn't do it again. Maybe that is why, as a reaction to that, I am very unpunctual!

My mother wasn't Jewish, but they became serious and my father proposed to her. However, she had to convert before they could marry. I think my mother started learning to become Jewish in about 1930 and she passed all her exams. By 1933, Hitler had come to power and towards the end of that year, she was fully converted so they could get married.

The actual wedding was in the huge Königsberg Synagogue, which is quite a famous one. It was destroyed on *Kristallnacht* (the Night of Broken Glass), but it has been rebuilt recently and was consecrated again in 2018. The Russians reconstructed a near replica of the original synagogue. I'm not sure why they did that but, perhaps, it was a case of a guilty conscience. My parents didn't have any guests at their wedding because the Nazis wouldn't allow them to come, and there were armed Nazi guards inside the synagogue. Aside from the rabbi, they did have two witnesses, Hugo Herrmann, my grandfather, and his brother, Hans Herrmann. There are no photographs of the wedding. My parents told me the Nazis wouldn't permit photography, as they didn't want to encourage anything. It is surprising that they allowed them to get married at all.

How my parents met and married

17 My mother, 1929

18 My mother was a beautiful young lady

19 Office party to celebrate the 30th anniversary of Steinberg's My mother Gretchen is sitting in the centre of the front row

20 My mother on the right with a friend, 1930

21 Aunt Margarete and Uncle Walter Schultz's wedding, July 1937.
My maternal grandfather Ludwig is on the left and Uncle Fritz is on the right.

Chapter 3

My father's escape to the Kitchener Camp

After the Nuremberg Laws were passed in 1935, which deprived Jews of their citizenship and rights, boycotts against Jews increased. Over time, Jews weren't allowed to work or to own businesses and the Nazis requisitioned whatever businesses they had. By 1938, my father's business had closed, so he volunteered at the local Zionist office to help people with visa applications. By then, many people were realising that something terrible was happening and wanted to leave Germany. However, they had to get visas for whichever country they wanted to go to.

I was told that one day, around June 1939, my father had a visit from one of the directors of this Zionist office. They told him that they just had notification that the Nazis were going to round up some people who would probably be sent to a concentration camp, and that he was on the list. They advised him to leave immediately. My father told them that he couldn't possibly leave, as he had a wife and child in Königsberg. Eventually, they convinced him that they would look after us, so he got ready to leave and packed a few things together.

In fact, the Nazis did come along. I don't know if it was that night, but my father was still there and he hid in the back bedroom. The Nazis asked my mother where my father was and she replied, "Oh, he's just gone out for a walk." She must have sounded very convincing as they said, "Okay, we'll come back later or tomorrow," and they left.

Through working in the visa office, my father heard about the Kitchener Camp scheme, which was set up with the help of the Central British Fund (CBF), now known as World Jewish Relief (WJR), to rescue mainly German and Austrian male refugees. They also helped Czechoslovakian and Hungarian refugees. It was a transit camp which was set up in Kent in England, for Jewish men aged between 17 and 45, to give them visas for onward journeys.

Jews were applying for visas for anywhere that would take them in, such as America, England and Holland. My father was already in the process of applying for visas for England. The idea was that these young men would go to the Kitchener Camp and stay there for two or three weeks, or however long it took, to go onwards to these other countries to safety.

My father was helped by the Zionist office in Königsberg to travel to Berlin, where they had an administrative office. We assume he got a train from Königsberg, through the 'Polish Corridor,' straight to Berlin. Then from Berlin, he went across to Hamburg and travelled by train to the Hook of Holland, where he

22 Me with my mother and father, September 1938

got on a boat to Harwich, and from there, a train to London. He then travelled to the Kitchener Camp in Sandwich, Kent and arrived there on 13 July 1939. The journey took about two days.

The Kitchener Camp was originally a First World War army camp. It was named after Lord Kitchener, the Secretary of State for War during the First World War. The camp housed around 4,000 male refugees in numerous single storey wooden huts, each holding about 40 men. The British Government didn't provide any money, but they did provide the camp. The CBF got money together from American and British Jewry, which they used for the men to refurbish the camp. Many of the men at the camp were skilled workers such as plumbers, plasterers and electricians. The men got paid 6d a week for their work, which is equivalent to 2.5 pence today. This was a very small amount in those days and might have bought my father a packet of cigarettes, as he was a smoker. When they left Germany, they were only allowed to take the equivalent of about 10 shillings or 50p!

In the camp, they had a post office, a cinema and a synagogue. They formed their own orchestra and had football teams. They also learned to speak English. My father had a sort of basic, schoolboy English when he arrived, but he became quite fluent. He was very good really, because he was 34 when he came to England, and it's not easy to pick up a foreign language at that age. Some of my parents' contemporaries never even learned English. He was a bit of a poet and wrote loads of poems, first in German and then later in English.

Danny Herman

```
Heiss geliebter Danimann!
Sieh' mich einmal freundlich an
Heut' an Deinem Ehrentage,
And'renfalls ich's garnicht wage,
Dir hiermit zu gratulieren.
Hab' ja Angst vor Deinen Vieren,
Womit oft mich hast bedacht!
Habe heut' drum mitgebracht
Eine Max und Moritz - Uhr,
Denn ich hoffe, durch die Tour
Wirst verlernen Du die Mucken,
Wenn auf diese Uhr tust gucken
Und an Max und Moritz denken!
Will auch noch ein Küsschen schenken
Und Dir gleich mal leise sagen,
Zeige stets Dein gut' Betragen
Bei den Eltern und so weiter,
Immer freundlich, froh und heiter!
Bleib' gesund bis 100 Jahr,
Dann wirst's schaffen, nicht? ganz klar!!!




Königsberg (Pr), den 15. September 1938.
```

23 A poem my father wrote for my 3rd birthday

Dear beloved Danny-man,
Look at me kindly if you can,
On this your special day of joy,
Or else I'll hardly dare, my boy,
To say "congrats" to you this way.
Be fearful of those fours, I say,
Which often make you think of me!
And so I've brought you presently,
A Max and Moritz clock, you'll learn,
(I'm hoping, as you watch it turn),
To put aside your sulks and strops,
When you look upon this clock,

> *And think of Max and Moritz too.*
> *I also send a kiss for you,*
> *And gently tell you, man-to-man;*
> *Always act the best you can,*
> *To your parents and whoever,*
> *Always friendly, cheerful, clever.*
> *Stay healthy 'til your hundredth year.*
> *Dan can do it, right? No fear!*

My father helped to build the roads at the Kitchener Camp and then after war was declared, he helped to fill sandbags to protect hospitals and similar buildings. The camp wasn't a prison. The men were not confined and were allowed to go out, such as to the local pubs or bars, with the sixpence they'd earned. They also worked for local farmers and other people, so earned a bit of extra money that way. My father stayed there until the end of December 1939.

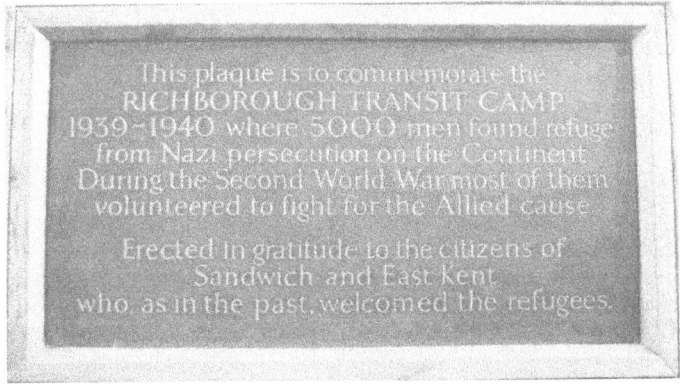

24 The plaque in Sandwich, Kent commemorating the Kitchener Camp, also referred to as the Richborough Transit Camp

25 Lord Kitchener featured in the well-known recruitment poster for the British Army

```
THE KITCHENER CAMP REVIEW.

The Journal of the Kitchener Camp for Refugees
at Richborough, near Sandwich, Kent.
No. 9.                    (New Series)                November, 1939.

THE DIRECTOR'S MESSAGE.

    Events have moved swiftly since last I addressed a message,
through the medium of this journal, to the men of the Camp, and the
tides have been as trying for those inside the Kitchener Camp as they
have been for those outside.

    Through all these difficulties the morale and spirit has been
high, and the eagerness of the majority to show their appreciation
to this country has been one of the highlights since the outbreak
of war.

    A large number of men have played their parts in National Service
efforts throughout Kent, performing such tasks as sand-bag filling,
air raid shelter making, trench digging and farming, with an effic-
iency that has won the approbation of all those for whom they have
worked, and now the opportunity has been given them of doing vital
National Service they have come forward in their thousands to place
themselves at the service of this country.

    For ten months I have had the privilege of leading the great
family at Richborough, and when the cloak of leadership falls from my
shoulders on to those of another I shall have the satisfaction of
knowing that I am handing over a body of men of whom any leader might
well be proud. I know that whatever task they may be called upon to
perform, whatever the nature of the service they may be called upon to
give to this country, they will never be found wanting.

    What may well be my last official message, must, therefore, con-
tain an expression of deep appreciation for the loyalty and for the
friendship which has been given to me since the beginning of February.

    A famous English admiral once sent what is now a famous
message to his men, and I, in all modesty, send a similar message now
I expect that all men of the Kitchener Camp will always do their
duty.
```

26 The November 1939 issue of the *Kitchener Camp Review*, which was a monthly journal

27 a, b, c My father's registration documents collated by the German Jewish Aid Committee

©WJR archive photos of Kitchener Camp. All rights reserved.

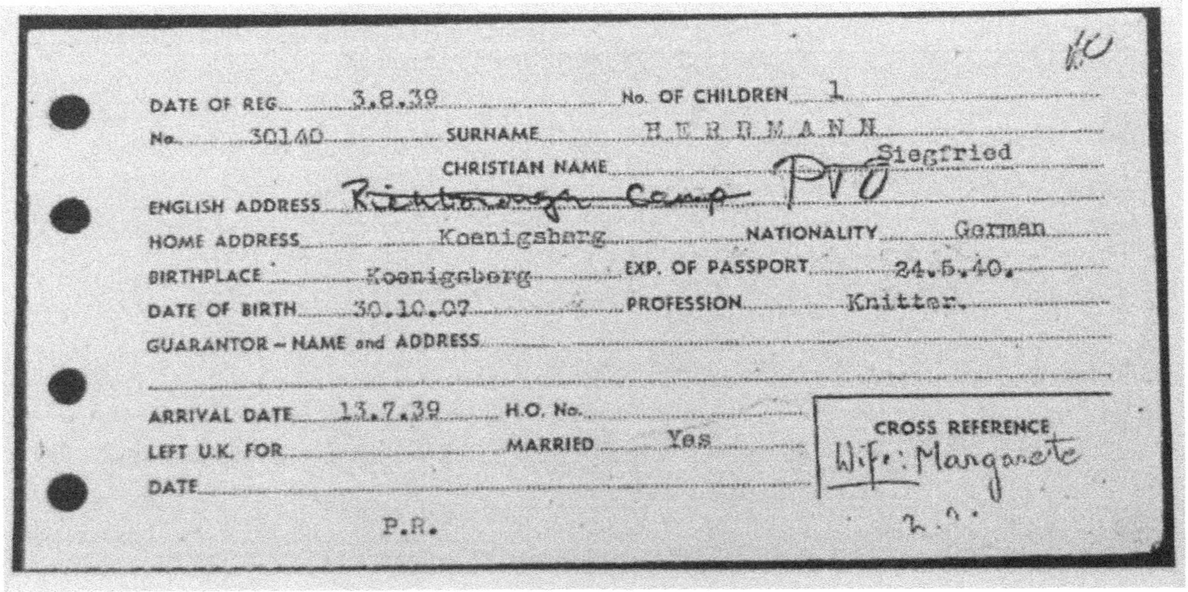

DATE OF REG. 3.8.39　　SURNAME HERRMANN　　No. OF CHILDREN 1

No. 30140　　CHRISTIAN NAME Siegfried

ENGLISH ADDRESS Richmond Camp PVD

HOME ADDRESS Koenigsberg　　NATIONALITY German

BIRTHPLACE Koenigsberg　　EXP. OF PASSPORT 24.5.40.

DATE OF BIRTH 30.10.07　　PROFESSION Knitter.

GUARANTOR – NAME and ADDRESS

ARRIVAL DATE 13.7.39　　H.O. No.

LEFT U.K. FOR　　MARRIED Yes

DATE

P.R.

CROSS REFERENCE
Wife: Margarete
2.c..

1, CAMPBELL RD, LONGSIGHT,
MANCHESTER 13

2 January Reshulaus ee a Laws, 4/5/46
See Ald. de Nu

6.12.45 2½ MOFFETT RD, RD, WEST DERBY
LIVERPOOL 12

11.3.46 35 BRENTSWIDGE RD, FALLOWFIELD
MANCHESTER 14

My father's escape to the Kitchener Camp

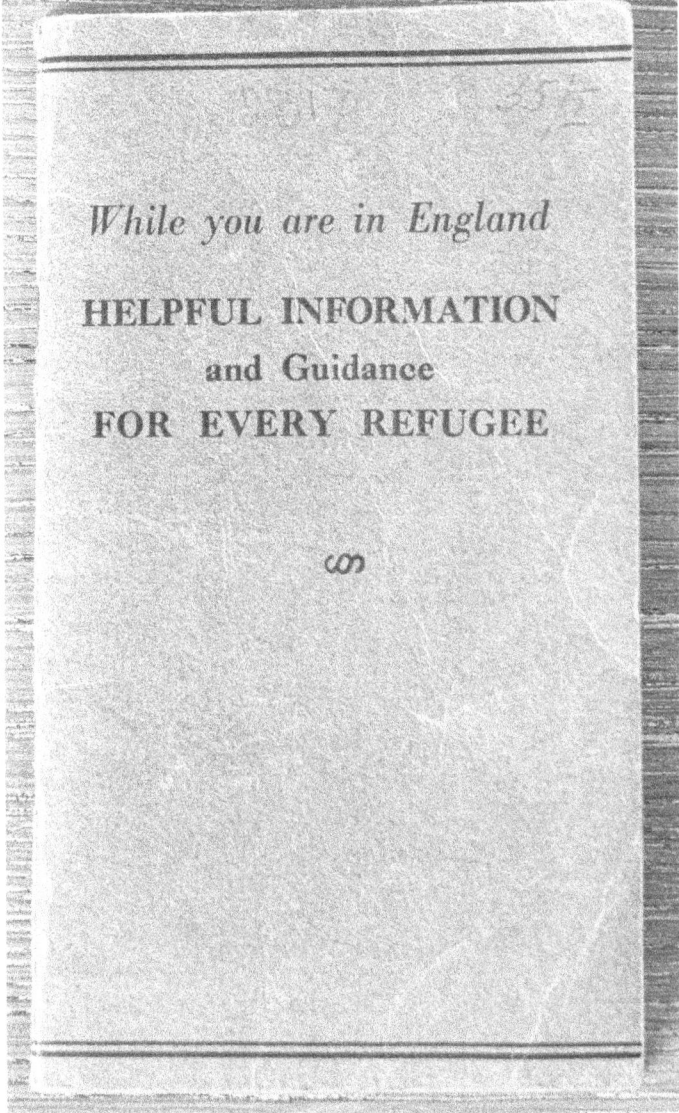

28 My father's refugee 'rule book'

SPECIAL

KITCHENER CAMP, RICHBOROUGH.

Name ...... HERMHNA SUGINER

Present Address
Gegenwärtige Adresse ......

Registration No.
at Bloomsbury House
Eingetragen im
Bloomsbury House unter Nr. 50440

Issued by
Herausgegeben von

THE GERMAN JEWISH AID COMMITTEE

Bloomsbury House, Bloomsbury St.,
London, W.C.1

In conjunction with
In Verbindung mit

THE JEWISH BOARD OF DEPUTIES

Woburn House

to give useful information and
friendly guidance to all Refugees

Dieses Buchlein bezweckt, allen
Flüchtlingen als nützliche Informationsquelle und freundlicher
Ratgeber zu dienen.

29 Page 1 of the 'rule book'

The TOLERANCE AND SYMPATHY of Britain and the British Commonwealth

THE traditional tolerance and sympathy of Britain and the British Commonwealth towards the Jewish community which every British Jew appreciates profoundly. On his part he does all in his power to express his loyalty to Britain and the British Commonwealth, in word and in deed, by personal service and by communal effort.

This loyalty comes first and foremost, and every Refugee should realise how deeply it is felt.

The Jewish Community in Britain will do its very utmost to welcome and maintain all Refugees, to educate their Children, to care for the Aged and the Sick—and to assist in every possible way in creating new homes for them overseas. A great many Christians, in all walks of life, have spontaneously associated themselves with this work. All that we ask from you in return is to carry out to your utmost the following lines of conduct. Regard them, please, as **duties to which you are in honour bound**:

Die Toleranz und Sympathie von Gross-Britannien und des Britischen Staatenbundes

DIE althergebrachte Toleranz Gross-Britanniens und des Britischen Staatenbundes und ihre Sympathie den Juden gegenüber wird von jedem britischen Juden zutiefst gewürdigt. In Wort und Tat, durch persönliche Dienste und gemeinsame Anstrengungen tut er seinerseits alles, was in seiner Macht steht, um seiner Loyalität zu Gross-Britannien und dem Britischen Staatenbund Ausdruck zu verleihen.

Diese Loyalität kommt zu allererst, und jeder Flüchtling sollte einsehen, wie tief sie empfunden wird.

Die Jüdische Gemeinde in Gross-Britannien wird ihr Äusserstes tun, um alle Flüchtlinge aufzunehmen und zu unterhalten, ihre Kinder zu erziehen, für die Alten und Kranken zu sorgen—und ihnen in jeder möglichen Weise behilflich zu sein, neue Heimstätten in überseeischen Ländern zu schaffen. Eine grosse Anzahl von Christen aus allen Schichten der Bevölkerung hat sich mit uns zu dieser Aufgabe zusammengeschlossen. Wir verlangen von Ihnen dafür dass Sie sich in Ihren Benehmen getreuestens nach den folgenden Regeln richten.

30 Pages 10–11 of the 'rule book'

1. Spend your spare time immediately in learning the English language and its correct pronunciation.

2. Refrain from speaking German in the streets and in public conveyances and in public places such as restaurants. Talk halting English rather than fluent German—and *do not talk in a loud voice*. Do not read German newspapers in public.

3. Do not criticise any Government regulations, nor the way things are done over here. Do not speak of "how much better this or that is done in Germany". It may be true in some matters, but it weighs as nothing against the sympathy and freedom and liberty of England which are now given to you. Never forget that point.

4. Do not join any Political organisation, or take part in any political activities.

5. Do not make yourself conspicuous by speaking loudly, nor by your manner or dress. The Englishman greatly dislikes ostentation, loudness of dress or manner, or unconventionality of dress or manner. The Englishman attaches very great importance to modesty, under-statement, and quietness of dress and manner. He values good manners far more than he values the

Betrachten Sie das Folgende bitte als Ehrenpflichten:

1. Verwenden Sie Ihre freie Zeit unverzüglich zur Erlernung der englischen Sprache und ihrer richtigen Aussprache.

2. Sprechen Sie nicht deutsch auf der Strasse, in Verkehrsmitteln oder sonst in der Öffentlichkeit, wie z.B. in Restaurants. Sprechen Sie lieber stockend englisch als fliessend deutsch—und sprechen Sie nicht laut. Lesen Sie keine deutschen Zeitungen in der Öffentlichkeit.

3. Kritisieren Sie weder Bestimmungen der Regierung noch irgendwelche englischen Gebräuche. Sprechen Sie nicht davon, "um wieviel besser dies oder das in Deutschland getan wird". Es mag manchmal wahr sein, aber es bedeutet nichts gegenüber der Sympathie und Freiheit Englands, die Ihnen jetzt gewährt werden. Vergessen Sie dies niemals.

4. Treten Sie weder einer politischen Organisation bei, noch nehmen Sie sonst Anteil an politischen Bewegungen.

5. Benehmen Sie sich nicht auffallend durch lautes Sprechen, durch Ihre Manieren oder Kleidung. Dem Engländer missfallen Schaustellungen, auffallende oder nichtkonventionelle Kleidung und Manieren.

31 Pages 12–13 of the 'rule book'

Chapter 4

My father's letters to Walter

My father wrote several letters to my mother's brother, Walter, whom he was able to contact again after the war. I have these letters, which were written between April and August 1946. They describe the time when he, then my mother and I, came to England and about our lives later on. He was very organised, and he used very thin paper to write on, keeping carbon copies. Paper was in short supply, so he wrote on both sides. I didn't know about the letters until my father died on 15 February 1979, as my mother kept all the papers. After my mother died in 2007, I went through everything and I translated the letters.

This letter to Uncle Walter is dated 4 July 1946. It explains exactly how my father left Königsberg just two months before the outbreak of war and how he got to the Kitchener Camp. He describes how there were 40 men to a hut, with 20 beds down each side, and the conditions were not marvellous. I find this letter very emotional.

'I experienced most curious feelings when, on the 12 July 1939, I left Germany together with a group of

32 Uncle Walter

My father's letters to Walter

```
                                              S.Herrmann
                                          Breatbridge Road,
                                          Manchester, 14.
                                          England.
                                                     .8.1948
Mr. & Mrs. W. Schulz,
(20) HAMELN/We.
Falkestr.11
Staatshochbauamt
Germany.
British Zone.
```

Meine sehr Lieben!

Heute gilt mein Brief in erster Reihe Dir, lieber Walter.
Gretchen hat ihren Brief schon vor einigen Tagen geschrieben,
selbst hatte es immer von einem Tag zum anderen verschoben, weil
ich mich sehr strapaziert fühlte. Augenscheinend ist mir das zwei
Wochen lange Nichtstun nicht gut bekommen, und denn – schon bei-
nahe an dem Nichtstun gewoehnt – hatte ich mich wieder in die
Arbeit hineinzufinden. Ihr wisst ja, dass es schwer ist, eine
Maschine wieder in Gang zu bringen, wenn sie eine Zeit lang un-
benutzt in der Ecke gestanden hat. Der Aufwand an Energien beim
Wiederankurbeln ist hier doppelt gross. – Also mein lieber Walter
Dein Geburtstag steht vor der Türe und gibt mir nach sieben langen
Jahren zum ersten Mal wieder die Moeglichkeit, Dir meine Gratulat.
on zu übermitteln. Ich glaube, ich brauche nicht die vielen guten
Wünsche alle einzeln aufzuzählen, die ich für Dich auf dem Herzen
habe. Ich moechte Dir und Gretchen vor allem gute Gesundheit
wünschen, unbeugsame Kraft des Koerpers und der Willens für die
bevorstehenden harten Wintermonate und weiter recht viel Freude an
Deinem Beruf. Ich moechte heute wiederholen, was ich Dir vor 7
Jahren geschrieben habe und was seinen Sinn nicht verloren hat
trotz der veraenderten Zeiten oder was vielleicht gerade wegen der
veraenderten Zeiten einen neuen Sinn gewonnen hat:

 Dies mein Wunsch für Dich nun sei,
 Bleib auch Du für immer frei
 Von dem Geiste der Verneinung –
 Halt' Dich fern von andrer Meinung.
 Denn Du hast es selbst gesehen,
 Dass noch immer lag geschehen,
 Was Du selbst Dir vorgenommen.
 Wenn Du nicht zu hoch erklommen
 Deiner Wünsche Stufen hast.
 Niemals moegst Du Lebenslast
 Allzu peinvoll, lästig spüren,
 Oeffne niemals Tor und Türen
 Boeser Leute oder Misamut.
 Sieh – es scheinet mir gewiss gut,
 Dass ein Fehlschlag sich mal zeigt,
 Dass nicht Mut sich übersteigt.
 Und in diesem Sinne schliessend,
 Dich und auch Dein Fraeuchen grüssend,

33 One of my father's letters to his brother-in-law, Walter

about 120 men of mixed ages (18-40 years). It was not that certain feeling of dejection, nor was it sadness and probably not even hate, which tends to get hold of people when they find themselves deprived of their country, their relatives, their friends, their possessions and their homes as they are expelled into exile from where, in general, they hope to be allowed to return one day. No, I knew that there was no return for me and that I, therefore, would have to suppress, under any circumstances, such feelings if they should ever venture to overcome me. It was the sense of fear, the sensation of a man who is running for his life, and the tremendously frightening worry of whether my family would be able to follow me in time; would I manage to earn the upkeep of my family without being dependent on the help of strangers; and altogether, what does the future hold in store for us?

Fortunately, there was no need for me to worry about my parents, my sister and her family and my wife's family because I believed them all to be safe and secure. Had I known or anticipated their fate, all my strength would probably have collapsed. As it was, there remained solely the feeling of being torn apart and the sad, yet somewhat consoling certainty that, at least, it was possible to exchange letters. At the same time, however, I knew that I had to keep back these thoughts as much as possible in order not to despair.

After crossing the German/Belgian border and then the Channel on 13 July 1939, I arrived at the Kitchener Camp straight into completely strange surroundings, to be greeted by thousands of fellow sufferers and the official English leaders. I suddenly had the encouraging feeling that perhaps, after all, a new life had begun for me, promising some happiness, despite all the hardships and difficulties; that it could be worthwhile to direct all our remaining strengths into a challenging struggle for this future life. Suddenly, bright sunshine seemed to break through the clouds after heavy thunderstorms, and then my hopes were actually realised and later the darkest clouds of all, the separation from my family, disappeared at last.

Very quickly and with great enthusiasm, I managed to adjust to camp life, to sharing a hut with 40 comrades of different backgrounds and education, having all meals jointly with hundreds of men, to the heavy manual work in the fields and the gardens, the construction of camp roads, and trying to speak a foreign language during occasional contact with Englishmen outside the camp. All that was so terribly new and needed some considerable ability to adapt oneself. It also demanded a considerable amount of energy, but it made me look to the future with pleasurable anticipation.'

And then he goes on to say,

'During those months I learned a great deal. I learned how to use my physical strength sparingly, how to lead a communal life without neglecting or giving up my individual inclinations and how to achieve contentment, to a certain degree, in spite of limited means at my disposal and food rationing with 6d (about 30 pfennigs) pocket money per week.'

Chapter 5

My arrival in England

Just after my father left for the Kitchener Camp, my mother was left to organise our journey to England. This was around 20 July 1939 and, at that stage, she still hadn't heard from the British Embassy about the success, or otherwise, of her visa application. So towards the end of August, she decided to go, personally, to the embassy with me. As she arrived, the embassy was closing, but my mother somehow managed to push to the front of the queue and gain entry. The official came back not only with passports, but with visas as well!

My mother and I made the same journey as my father had made, on one of the last boats over to England. When we set off from Königsberg, I had only a little suitcase with me. My mother apparently told me that we were going on a nice seaside holiday, so I packed my bucket and spade and my teddy bear, as a four-year-old would do. However, I have been told this teddy bear fell overboard when we were on the boat from the Hook of Holland to England, and there was no way of retrieving it. I often think about this bear and even told a fictional story at my mother's 95th birthday party about a giant-sized teddy bear, which we had in the house from when my children were young. I claimed it had been rescued when it was dropped overboard by a little boy and had been travelling around the country until it ended up coming back to us for the party!

We arrived in England on 31 August 1939, three days before war was declared. We travelled to the Kitchener Camp where there was an area for women. Originally, it wasn't meant for women and children at all, but they did create one hut for them. However, the conditions were terrible in this hut and my mother didn't like us being there. My father managed to borrow money, which he later repaid, so we could stay at a bed and breakfast for a week.

The camp was near the seaside, so there were many bed and breakfasts available, such as one would find in Blackpool or St Annes. He booked one of these for us, as we were still feeling the effects of our long and tiring journey. The room cost about £3 for the week, which was all my father could afford. I celebrated my fourth birthday there on 15 September 1939, and then we returned to the camp for the remaining two weeks of our stay. One of the conditions for getting the visa was that the applicant had to have a job. My mother had been able to do this with the help of the Quakers. They helped her to get a position as a domestic servant (housekeeper) with a family in Didsbury, South Manchester, and that was due to start on 1 October 1939.

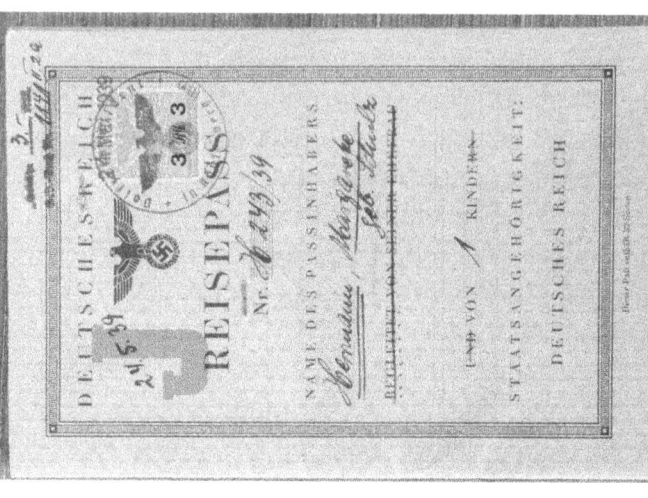

34 a and b My mother's German passport including our visa for travel to the UK. It was issued just before war broke out.

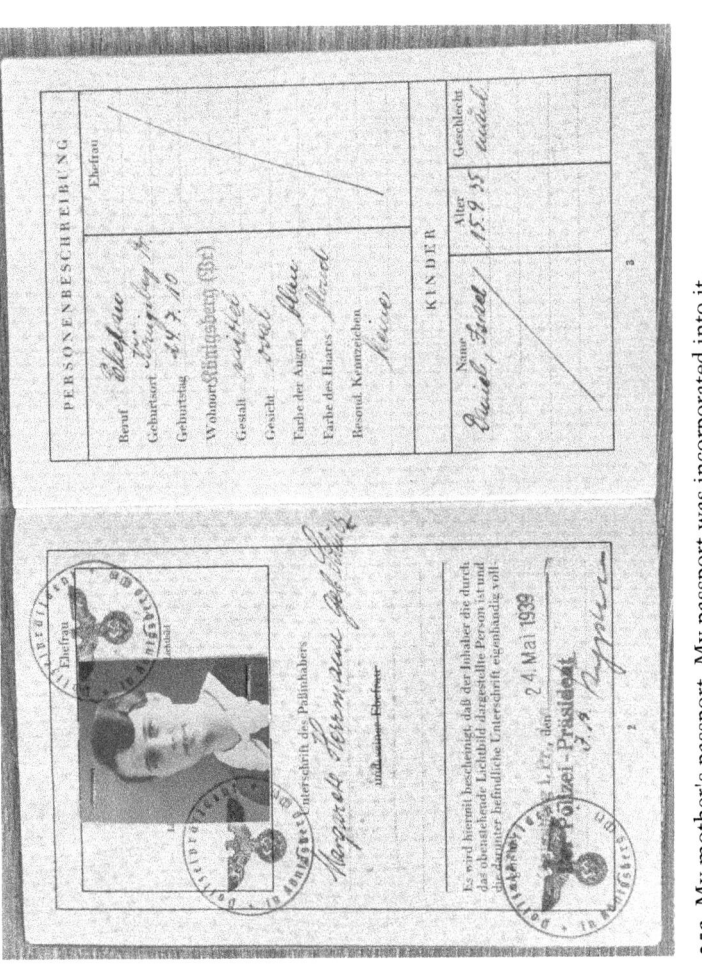

35a My mother's passport. My passport was incorporated into it.

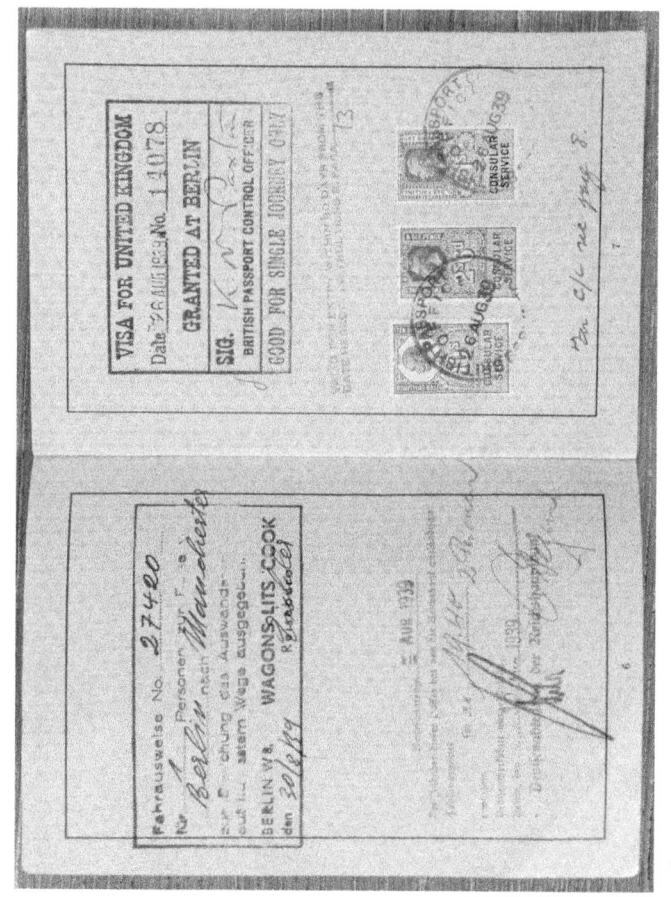

My arrival in England

My father writes in his letter to Uncle Walter,

'Gretchen and Danny arrived in London on 31 August 1939, after a very difficult journey with many anxious moments and a breathtaking escape. I organised the last part of their journey from London so that they arrived at the recently opened Kitchener Camp for Women on 1 September, which was for me a triumph of utter happiness and joy!

Two days later, our unbridled celebrations were somewhat dampened and suppressed by the events of that time. WAR! Those first few days and weeks, at the beginning of the war, were perhaps my most terrible experiences in England, despite many other frightening events later on during the course of the war.

There were approximately 3,300 people crowded together in one quarter of a square kilometre. Three quarters of them were haunted by the nerve-racking thought that they would be separated from their families for an uncertain period of time, at least the duration of the war. They did not know then that they would never see them again, and that their families could lose their lives in the gas chambers of the concentration and extermination camps, as the victims of soulless and bestial men.

Those camp inmates became restless and nervous, and it was inevitable that this restlessness was transmitted to those who were not affected. Life in the camp gradually became a torment, especially in the women's section, which was separated from the main camp. Life became almost unbearable. I managed to borrow a little money from friends which enabled me to arrange a week's full board and lodging for Gretchen and Danny with an English couple in a small town nearby. There it was possible for her to pull herself together and gather strength for her job as a domestic in Manchester, which was due to start on 1st October.'

In the meantime, my father hadn't got a job. When my mother got to Manchester, she started looking for a job for him. Eventually she found one, but that didn't start until 2 January 1940 so, in the meantime, he stayed at Kitchener Camp doing all sorts of odd jobs.

36 a and b My parents in 1939

Chapter 6

My foster family

My mother's job as a domestic was at the home of the French Consul in Manchester, who had a Russian wife. They lived on Kinnaird Road in Didsbury in a big old Victorian house, opposite where the Christie Hospital is today. She described herself as a 'cook general'. She really didn't like her time there and thought she was very badly treated. The husband was fine, but the wife wasn't. They used to do a lot of entertaining and my mother did all the cooking for them. For some reason, the guests used to come into the kitchen to congratulate the cook and were all very friendly, but the lady of the house didn't like it. She wanted to imply that she had done all the cooking herself!

Part of the condition for me getting a visa to travel to England with my mother was that I had to have foster parents. So before we left, my mother had written to lots of places including the Society of Friends, the Quakers, who were on Mount Street in Manchester. At that time, the Quakers were getting many letters and, of course, they needed someone to translate

My foster family

them because they were in German. A certain lady, a Mrs Schäfer, used to translate these letters. She and her husband lived on Spring Bridge Road, which is off Wilbraham Road in Chorlton. Mr Schäfer was Jewish but his wife was not, and they did not really involve themselves with the Jewish community.

One day, Mrs Schäfer came across a letter from my mother explaining that she had a son, me, and he needed a home. She said, "I know that family. We've got to do something for them." It turned out that she knew of the Herrmann family, as she had come from Königsberg herself, but probably much earlier on, in the early 1930s. Therefore, she made efforts to find me a foster place.

The Quakers put an appeal out for people to foster refugee children. That same day, an English couple came into the Quakers' building on Mount Street and said, "We're looking to foster a young child, have you got anyone suitable?" And, because Mrs Schäfer happened to be there that day, she introduced them to me, by showing them a photograph. I must have been very cute because they said they would help me! Their names were Elsie and Sydney Holmes.

At that time, children who came over on the Kindertransport had to have a guarantor who would pay £50 per child, which was a lot of money in those days. I don't know whether the Holmes had to pay that for me as well. Sydney was a retired dentist and Elsie was a primary school teacher. She was quite a bit younger than him. They lived in a place called Broadbottom,

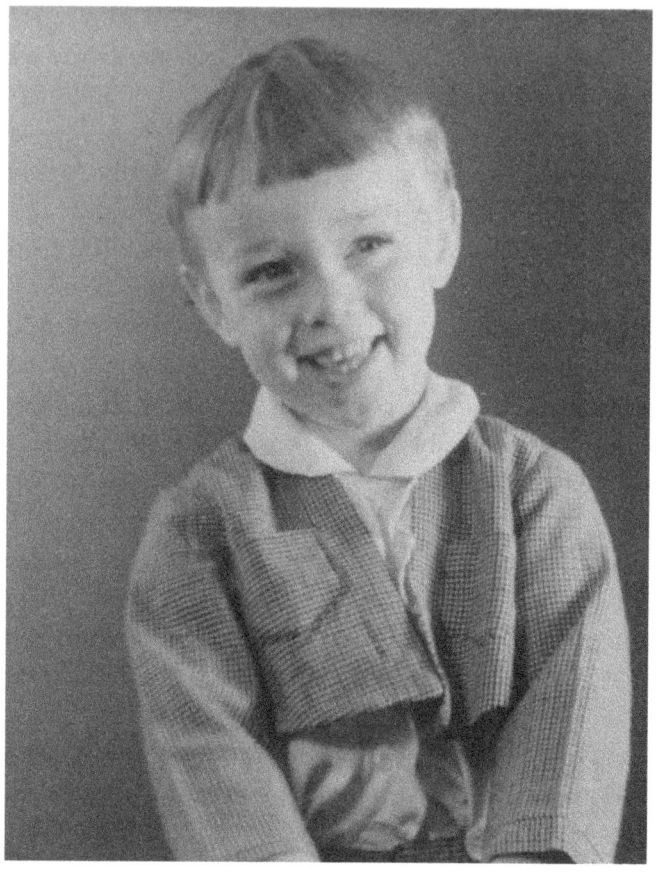

37 Me aged four

which is near Hyde in Greater Manchester. They didn't have any children of their own, but they had adopted a son, Reg, who was about 28. I think he was a couple of years younger than my mother.

When my mother started work at Kinnaird Road, she took me to live with the Holmes family. I can

My foster family

remember they lived in a small, semi-detached house on a main road, and a bit further along the road was the primary school where Mrs Holmes taught. I was just over four years old at the time, and she used to take me to school every day, which is where I learned English. I was with them for about six months.

The only memory I have of Broadbottom itself is that the school was on the top of a very steep slope leading down to the main road. I remember one day cutting my eye badly and having stitches, after falling down this grass slope. I also remember I was badly knock-kneed when I was that age, so they must have taken me to the doctor, and I had to go to bed at night with a plaster cast. The cast didn't go all the way around my leg, but it held my leg in a straight position to reposition my knee. The other thing I remember from my time with the Holmes family was eating nuts, as they were vegetarians!

The Holmes' son, Reg, was quite a character. He should have been called up for service in the Second World War, but he was a conscientious objector. When I first met him, he was the warden of the YHA (Youth Hostels Association) in Delamere. His wife was called Mabel and she worked at the Delamere School. They bought a 300-year-old cottage near Flaxmere, on the outskirts of Delamere. After the war, he left the YHA and joined the railways. He became a signalman at Delamere Station, which only had three or four trains a day passing through, so not very hard work! He taught himself Italian in between trains, and he also learned German and Welsh. Reg was able to speak to my parents in German. When Reg was in his 90s, he used to be a 'caller' for country dancing at the village hall. He used to ride around on a scooter and swim in the lake in Delamere Forest every day!

38 Reg and Mabel in Delamere Forest

39 My mother (far left) outside Reg and Mabel's cottage in Delamere

40 L-R: Mabel Holmes, Sydney Holmes, my father and Elsie Holmes, 1961

My mother was not happy at all working at Kinnaird Road because of the way the lady of the house bullied her. She had to work very hard, cooking and cleaning the six bedroom house, and she only had a few hours off. I think the boss didn't mind her having a half-day off, but she needed more than half a day to get across town to see me. Now you could probably drive there in 40 minutes.

My foster family

I think my mother was only allowed to visit me once a month, and not at all in the first two months, so that I could settle in with my foster parents. That was probably a good thing because I would have been upset wouldn't I?

While my mother had her few hours off a week, she started looking for jobs for my father and eventually, she found him one in a knitting factory in Salford. As my father had studied textile engineering at college, he knew all about knitting. He travelled from the Kitchener Camp to Manchester for an interview around November 1939 and started the job on 2 January 1940. He came up to Manchester then to join us, which was very good. I don't think my father stayed at Kinnaird Road, but he would have visited.

After about six months or so, things got a bit difficult for my foster family and unfortunately, they couldn't foster me any longer. I don't think it was because I was particularly badly behaved, as none of the stories I've read suggested that. I think the problems were financial, so I returned to my mother and she had to give up her job to look after me. My parents and I went to live in a single furnished bedsit, with three of us in one room and a shared bathroom. My mother then decided that we should find another place. This was in 1940, so my mother was 30 and my father was 36. I would have been four, nearly five by then.

Chapter 7

Moving to Mabfield Road

My mother found us rented accommodation, which was a terraced house on Mabfield Road in Fallowfield, and she got a new job nearby. On the other side of the road, there was a block of flats called Appleby Lodge. She worked there as a housekeeper for a Swiss gentleman who had a grown-up daughter, and he treated my mother very well. I believe we rented house number 44 on Mabfield Road because I had occasion to walk past it during the Commonwealth Games in 2002. It is near Owens Park. My mother managed to supplement the small income she earned as a housekeeper by subletting some of the rooms in our house to three German Jewish girls in their late teens, also refugees. My father worked for about four or five months as a knitter and then, in May 1940, he was interned by government edict on the Isle of Man.

I went to a church primary school, which was about a three-quarter mile walk from our house on Mabfield Road. My mother walked with me but left me to my own devices for the last quarter mile, which would be unheard of today at the age of five. We were taught to knit at this primary school, making squares for blankets. I have forgotten how to do it now. Our class of four and five-year-olds were knitting squares for the teacher to sew together to make blankets for the soldiers in the war. All I remember of that primary school was the knitting.

Before my mother and I had travelled to England, she had organised our belongings to be sent there. Apparently, it was possible to send a container if you paid as much as the value of the contents as a penalty. There were restrictions as to what you could take in it. A Nazi official had to supervise and observe the packing to make sure you weren't taking any restricted items. I don't think they would have allowed you to take expensive items of jewellery or porcelain, or anything like that. However, I think my mother drew the long straw. An official watched her packing and detailed everything - every individual fork, knife, spoon and pair of scissors were listed.

When my mother eventually came to the silver plate, the family *seder* plate, the official said, "What's that?" to which she replied, "It's a religious item." Fortunately, he accepted that and said, "OK". That is how our silver *seder* plate was able to be sent in the container together with all the accessories. I suppose it must have looked very strange. We also had the spice container for *Havdalah*, which I later gave to our rabbinical grandson-in-law, Yacov, in Israel. We had one or two silver *bechers* and candlesticks, but the official seemed to overlook those and allowed us to put them in the container.

The other things in the container were my father's old bicycle, some bed linen, crockery and tablecloths. We also brought a set of garden furniture, but it wasn't like the current rattan style, or even plastic; it was made from wood. It consisted of a round wooden table that folded flat and had slats across it. Over the years, it got a bit worn and we put a Formica top on it. There were also two armchairs that folded up, and there was another small folding chair for me. It was like Goldilocks and the Three Bears, with the two big chairs and one little one! Amazingly, this furniture has survived at least 80 years, as I am not sure if it was new at the time. My daughter, Linda, has it all now.

We also took my very large cot, which had been used by other members of the family before me, so it could be almost 100 years old now! I slept in it until I was six or seven, as it was bigger than the cots they have in England. Then, years later, all our kids slept in it, and I repainted it for each new baby in our family.

The container came via Amsterdam with the help of my aunt and uncle, who were there when my mother sent it in 1939, as we didn't have an address in England at that time. My father's sister, Gretchen, her husband and her son, Gerhard, who was born in 1928, had all escaped to Holland in 1938. They had set up a small factory making gloves in what was a Jewish area in Amsterdam. They lived in two rented flats above the factory and our things were sent to that address. By the time the container arrived in Amsterdam, we had an address in Manchester, so it was redirected.

41 Itemised packing list for the container

```
                    H a n d g e p ä c k
                                                    5. Juni 1939

    Siegfried Israel Herrmann   Julchental 2  Koenigsberg Pr.


             1     1     Rasierspiegel
             2     1     P. Handschuhe
             1     2     Messer und Gabeln           1917    Silber
             1     2     Frühstücksmesser u.Gabeln     "       "
             1     3     Esslöffel                    "       "
             1     4     Teelöffel                    "       "
             1     2     Küchengabeln                 "       "
             1     1     Serviettenring (Kinder)    1904      "
             1     1     Weinbecher                   ?      )
     1   1   1     Pesachschae                        ?      )Kultgerät
     1   1   1     Sederschüssel mit Zubehoer       1925     )
     1   2   1     goldener Ehering                 1933
     1   2   1     Taschenmesser
```

42 Part of the itemised contents list for the container

I vaguely remember the container arriving in May 1940, which was just 10 days before Germany invaded Holland. I went with my mother to Salford Docks, now Salford Quays, to pick it up. We were able to use the contents for the house on Mabfield Road. The house was not furnished, and the only furniture we had was the folding garden table. The rest of the furniture was bits and pieces that people donated, and we used orange boxes as bedside tables.

My father writes in a letter to Uncle Walter:

'Fate continued to favour us. In the meantime, we learned that our goods and chattels, packed in chests and suitcases, had arrived in Holland. At that time, Holland was still neutral, so we were able to redirect everything to Manchester.

Although this meant new debts for us, which were quite substantial in relation to our lifestyle at that time, we were able to pay the transport cost with the help of friends here and relatives in Palestine. The goods arrived here just 10 days before the German troops invaded Holland.

We managed to rent an empty house quite cheaply and made a very cosy home of it with modest means at our disposal, and with the assistance of friendly, understanding English people who lent us some furniture. I even got involved in a little DIY, attempted some joinery to complete some of the furnishings, rather amateurish, but at least it gave me some encouragement.

However, the war began to cast its first shadows on us. The German invasion of Holland, Belgium and France meant that we no longer had postal communications with our relatives in Holland. Later on we did hear from them, albeit sporadically, either through the Red Cross or in a roundabout way through friends in

America. We could no longer deny the fact that the real war had begun and that the allies were not winning. War was being brought very close to us all, and actually we couldn't raise much enthusiasm for the progress we'd made with our private lives whilst the current situation existed.

Before we had time to turn around, suddenly the world was ablaze. Many refugees had arrived in the UK from Holland and Belgium, but our faint hopes that my parents and my sister and her family might have been amongst them were soon dashed. There then followed the capitulation of France and, in the wake of that, the internment of all enemy aliens here, if they had not already been interned at the beginning of the war. I, too, was one of them, having been of German nationality although like most refugees, I was recognised officially as a refugee from Nazi oppression. Gretchen, like most women, was not interned.'

Chapter 8

My father's internment

At the outbreak of the war, Austrians and Germans living in England had been classed as 'enemy aliens', as it was feared they could be spies. Initially, only a small number were considered high risk enough to intern, but by May 1940, things were getting tough in England and there was increasing hostility towards anybody German or Austrian. Prime Minister Winston Churchill then decided to intern thousands of 'enemy aliens'. Anybody who came from Germany, Austria and also Italy had to report to the police, including my father.

He was first of all sent to a grotty old mill in Bury which housed about 2,000 men. I can imagine a great big floor with hundreds of beds there. He was there for about two weeks, and then they were sent to a former holiday camp in Scotland. My father was quite shrewd because he volunteered to work in the kitchen, as he knew he'd get some food! They stayed in the camp for two or three weeks, before being taken to the Isle of Man.

For the internment camps in the Isle of Man, boarding houses were requisitioned and barbed wire was placed around the gardens. They had Nissen huts as well. My father was lucky, as he went to a boarding house where they only had a dozen people. He became the entertainment officer for his section and had to organise many activities.

About 27,000 to 28,000 men were interned in the end. One internment camp at Peel, which is on another side of the island, had a small section just for women and children. First the men were interrogated because everybody was classed as an 'enemy alien'. After they had been debriefed and the authorities decided that they weren't the enemy, they became 'friendly aliens'. Many of the internees were Jewish refugees. However, some of the internees were pro-Nazis as there were non-Jewish Germans living in England at the time who hadn't gone back home.

The men were sent to work for the local farmers all summer, picking and planting potatoes. They were allowed to take one or two potatoes and potatoes became the currency. It was one potato for a few cigarettes, or something like that. Most of these Jewish men had never worked in fields or had ever seen countryside.

My father describes his experiences in a letter to Uncle Walter on 22 April 1946:

'My very dearest, this is the first continuation of the report I began on 6 April 1946. It was on 4 July 1940, a dull and rainy day, when I suddenly found myself in a hastily improvised internment camp in Bury, a small

town near Manchester. A thousand thoughts raced through my head, threw me into a state of panic, and it was only because of great self-control and serious consideration that I, and my fellow internees, realised the need for these measures. There was not a single one amongst us who was not grateful from the bottom of our hearts to the English people and their government for granting us asylum in a safe haven. We hoped that we would be allowed, somehow, to apply our vigour in the struggle for justice and individual freedom. Once again, we saw ourselves deprived of this freedom.

As we did not know the government's decisions concerning our cases, and since we learned only later that they wanted to examine our political reliability, we became rather dejected. I became aware of my own homelessness for the first time, as well as that of us all. It was a fact that I had registered merely hypothetically until then, without being overcome by the feelings resulting from it because of the many events and happenings.

Everything that I had learned of Jewish history for the last few thousand years, I was now experiencing myself. I had been deprived of my German nationality, which I had acquired through my ancestors of many past generations. And all the same, I was now still regarded as a German citizen. These thoughts were suppressed by the worry about Gretchen, who was left on her own with the expense of running a house and supporting Danny, whose keep I had already been paying for the last three months.

Furthermore, I was depressed by the fact that we, more than 2,000 men, were obliged to sleep in large halls in old disused cotton mills, completely deprived of all comforts because this camp had been put together very quickly on a provisional basis. However, eventually I managed to pull myself together and I volunteered to work in the camp kitchen. I did so partly to drive away my gloomy thoughts and partly to ease my hunger, as I would be nearer the source of food! Unfortunately, our worries were increased by the rumour that we were to be transferred overseas. All the men were amazed and relieved when, about two weeks later, we found ourselves together again in a very nice holiday camp in Scotland. This was situated in the midst of wonderful mountains and magnificent forests.

After another two weeks, we received the first post from our relatives, and we thought that we had not been completely cut off from the rest of the world after all. After three weeks in Scotland, we were transferred yet again, this time by steamship on a glorious day in August to the Isle of Man, an island near the west coast of England in the Irish Sea, with beautiful and splendid scenery. We began to believe that we were at last approaching the end of our long ordeal. It would transpire later that our hopes were not in vain. In those days, there was a slogan circulating in England, 'Join the forces and see the world'. We changed it a little to say, 'Join the internees and see Great Britain.'

Whilst my father was interned, I remember how it was living through the Blitz with my mother at Mabfield Road in December 1940. We didn't have an air raid shelter as it was a terraced house, so there was no room for one. At the end of our road, on Wilmslow Road, there were these large Victorian houses that had big, spacious cellars. All the local community had to go into those cellars when there was an air raid, so we quite often spent the whole night in those dark, miserable cellars.

From Mabfield Road, it was about 200 yards to the cellars. When we heard the siren, we would have to rush and sprint down the road to the cellar. It wasn't a question of going to the end of the garden into a cellar. Then one day, we got bombed. I remember I came back to the house early in the morning after the bombing raid, when it was 'all clear'. The roof on the lean-to kitchen at the back of our house was smoking. The roof had more or less disappeared because a huge earthen ball had hit it. The only place it could have come from was the park. A bomb must have fallen and sent this earthen ball flying. It was amazing it hit us as we were at least 100 yards away. The landlord must have paid for the repairs.

My father didn't know about this bombing at the time. He later writes to Walter,

'Our house was hit three times and Gretchen and Danny had to spend most nights sleeping in a public air raid shelter for the next few months. This of course left its mark on their minds and their nerves, but fortunately, they have long since got over it.

In the internment camp, we only got brief and incomplete news reports as our relatives were not allowed to send detailed accounts of happenings

because of the danger of spies. This was probably quite good because otherwise we'd have had more problems to worry about, without being able to do anything about it.'

After seven months of internment, when all the interrogation had more or less been completed and internees had been sorted out between 'friend' and 'enemy', my father was given three options. He could stay on the Isle of Man until the end of the war planting potatoes and picking them, or join the Royal British Pioneer Corps, which a lot of the men did. However, I think many of them who went into the Pioneer Corps were single, and my father wanted to be with his family. Then there was the option for engineers or those who had industrial experience to go and work in munitions or aeroplane factories. He chose this option, having been a textile engineer.

My father thought he would be sent to Manchester, or he hoped he would be, but he was sent to Liverpool to work in a newly-built aeroplane factory called Napier's, using his skills on the lathes. They made Hawker Hurricane fighter aeroplanes, and he made the engines for them. In his letter to Walter, he says that he was released on 8 February 1941 and was fortunate to be one of the first internees to be released.

I always tell the story of how on my father's first day at the factory, his new Scouse friends said to him, "What's your name?" and he replied, "Siegfried." They said, "Oh, we can't call you that, that's far too German. We'll call you Fred." So everybody called him Fred throughout the war.

Chapter 9

Life in Liverpool during the war

After my father was released from the Isle of Man, my mother and I went to join him in Liverpool. Mum gave up her job in Manchester and we managed to find a semi-detached house on Lingmell Road in Liverpool, in a district called West Derby. I remember there was a big wide road nearby, which had trams running down the middle. We rented the house and eventually were able to negotiate to buy it. I think it cost £500. My father continued to work at Napier's.

In a letter to my uncle, he explains how he came to get us:

'I went there to visit Gretchen and Danny and two weeks later, I brought them over to Liverpool and rented rooms from a young woman with whom we're all still friendly today. And two weeks later, we moved to a wonderful furnished house with a big garden at the rear, at a very reasonable rent, not far from the factory in West Derby, a modern suburban district with beautiful parks at touching distance. Despite the daily struggles working in these factories, occasional night shifts and the artificial light, and despite the

restrictions imposed by the war, we spent a number of happy years in this house without any financial worries or any problems in feeding ourselves.'

My memory of life in Liverpool is that West Derby was not a particularly Jewish area, but my father wanted to live near where he was working. So we joined Greenbank Drive Synagogue in Liverpool, which is now a listed building that stands empty, as the Jews have moved away from there. I remember that during the war there was always a big crowd at the synagogue. There were a lot of American GIs there, Jewish Americans, and at six or seven years old, I used to chase them around asking for chewing gum!

I remember going to Hebrew classes at the synagogue. From the age of six or seven, I travelled there by myself on the tram, bus and on foot. I could not imagine this happening now. My parents didn't have a car, and the only form of transport they had was my father's bike, which I learnt to ride! I couldn't get on it properly because the crossbar was too high for me, which was very dangerous!

I remember on one Sunday morning, I was dreading going to Hebrew classes. I don't know why, but maybe I had not done my homework. I was probably only about eight or nine years old. My usual journey was to take a tram three or four stops, from where I caught a bus to Penny Lane and then another to class. However, that day I decided I would stop at Penny Lane, which was later immortalised by the Beatles. I spent the morning, from 10am until 1pm, wandering around that

Life in Liverpool during the war

area looking at the shops all on my own, and then went back. I never told my parents about it. They just assumed that I was going to class and doing well.

My first school in Liverpool was a Church of England school, about a mile from my home. I joined it in March 1941 and stayed until September 1942, by which time I was seven years old. Despite my limited knowledge of English, I did quite well and finished in the top three in my class in all subjects. Perhaps my parents didn't feel I was being sufficiently challenged as, for whatever reason, they transferred me to the local state primary school. It was around a two mile walk from home, which I walked there and back alone. It had twice as many pupils as my first school and I stayed there until December 1945.

I was very close to my mother and father. I remember my mother took me to Cubs. However, I only went for two weeks because I tore my trousers in the first and the second week, so my mother said that was it, I couldn't go any more!

In Liverpool, we had an Anderson air raid shelter in our garden. My father had to dig a deep hole and put this corrugated steel shell over the top of it. We never really went in, miserable things they were. Then we got a different shelter, an indoor one. It was a table shelter, probably 6 feet by 12 feet, and it took up most of the front part of the room after it had been installed. It was made of metal, so if there was an air raid, you could go underneath and if the house was hit, everything would fall on top of it. But it never happened to us.

I remember the house had quite a big garden with a lawn. However, it probably wasn't that big, just how it seemed to me then. Beyond the lawn was a little allotment, so my father grew vegetables and there were small fruit trees.

My father got some furniture for the house called 'utility' furniture. In those days, it was the only furniture you could buy and you had to have coupons for it. It was very basic and if you wanted anything different, you had to go to a second-hand shop. We wanted some second-hand furniture as well, so my parents took in lodgers to supplement their income. Two young men, who my father had met at work, shared a room in our three bedroom house. One was called Curt Catson, Katzenstein originally, and the other one was also a Curt, Curt Lieberman. After the war, he went to Santiago in Chile and we lost touch with him. But Curt Catson went to live in Birmingham and we were friends until he died, in around 2005.

My parents had the main bedroom, I had the small room and then the two boys had the other room. They stayed with us for a couple of years.

My mother never had a job in Liverpool as such, only looking after the lodgers. She used to make them meals and we all ate together. My mother would prepare a huge picnic meal, including sandwiches and drinks for when we went to the cinema. When it came to the weekends, we used to take the ferry across to Birkenhead, on the Wirral, and we would go to places like New Brighton.

We did take a couple of holidays. We went to a place called Llanfairfechan, which is in North Wales, a beach resort not far from Portmeirion. I remember we used to stay at a small bed and breakfast place. I think we went a couple of times.

My parents had refugee friends in Liverpool. I remember the German style of entertaining and socialising they did, where they used to go around to friends and have *kaffee und kuchen* (coffee and cakes). They always took me along because there was nowhere else to put me! I suppose it would have been difficult to afford babysitters. I was with them while they were having coffee and cake but then, when they were chatting, they'd put me in another room where I would read or play. That is how life progressed for us in Liverpool.

In May 1945, at the end of the war, after VE Day (Victory in Europe), we had a street party and that is where I ran my first race. It was a race with kids probably my age, which I managed to win, and they gave me a prize. It was a National Savings stamp, which was six pence, equivalent to 2.5 pence today! I didn't tell the AAA (Amateur Athletics Association) about this later on because they might have considered me to have run professionally, and amateurs were not allowed to be paid!

The road was quite wide, with houses down each side. There were lots of children on that street, and they had races for all age groups. They even had a race for the parents and my mother came second, but I think she fell over. She would have been 35 at the time. Then my father ran, but he didn't win.

Chapter 10

Moving to Manchester

My father was made redundant towards the end of the war, so he had to find a new job, which wasn't easy. It took him about four months, but he eventually got a job with a Jewish-owned textile company in Manchester city centre as an office manager. I'm not sure why he got it because he didn't have much experience in that field. I remember when my parents told me they were going to move to Manchester, I was very upset because I didn't want to leave.

Whilst my father had been looking for a job, it was fortunate that we had taken in some new lodgers, a couple of Norwegian seamen, to give us extra income. It must have been quite risky for them to be on the high seas in the war. I think they were called Antonson and Svenson. After the war when I was about 12 years old, they came to visit us in Manchester because their ship sailed into Salford docks, right down the Manchester Ship Canal. I was a quiet boy back then. They invited a friend and me to go on board at the dock and go to Liverpool. I can remember going on the boat, which was a cargo ship, and being allowed to wander around and look over the edge. It stopped in Liverpool somewhere, dropped us off and then carried on to where it was going. We got the train back. That was a great day out for us, a good adventure.

This is my father's recollection of our move to Manchester, as written to my Uncle Walter:

'It was going well for the Allies, so the first redundancies began in autumn of 1944. And because of the shortage of work, I was transferred to a different department where I had to work very hard, much harder than before. At the beginning of the New Year 1945, I was tired and exhausted from the excessively strenuous work. I was engaged on continuous night work. I was eventually very relieved when at the beginning of March, because of the shortage of work hours, they gave notice to terminate my employment. Having seen thousands before me being released, for the moment I was not particularly worried about the future because I hoped to find an interesting position in the textile industry. But then it took longer than I thought. I travelled to Manchester a few times, twice to London and apart from that to many other industrial places to make contacts.

By the beginning of May, when the war in Europe had come to an end, I had still not found a job. Fortunately, just after our young lodgers had left us, we let our room on a full board basis to two Norwegian officers of the Norwegian Merchant Navy, paying a very good rent so that we didn't have to touch our savings. Apart from that, they were very good company, and we were able to very quickly make friends with them and my unused time was also somewhat fulfilled. My main occupation at that time was writing letters to all possible companies.

At the end of May, it had to be a coincidence that, after I'd been walking the streets almost a month, a Manchester firm to which I had been recommended were looking for an office manager for a new business, and I got the job. So I had no choice but to find myself some lodgings in Manchester for the weekdays, which I found very quickly with some friends from Königsberg. It was the family of the oldest son of Julius Rawraway. We used to live with them early on in Königsberg, on Clarastrasse, actually living in one house. I would go to Liverpool every Friday night and spend the weekend with my family until Monday morning. And then, after five months, I'd had enough of this gypsy style of living. Gretchen, with her usual efficiency, didn't need long to look and only on the second day she found a suitable house, which we decided to buy coincidentally on my birthday, 30 October. That evening, therefore, we had two opportunities to celebrate.

We moved into the house on 18 December 1945, after I had sold the Liverpool house. The deal was only possible because of the mutual trust between both parties and the bridging loan on the house in Liverpool and the Manchester acquisition, which happened more or less simultaneously, leaving me with no money. On the other hand, I couldn't sell Liverpool without having secured a place to live in Manchester, so I had to take out a loan. Moreover, when you buy a house here, you have to take out a mortgage and together with interest, pay it off over a number of years, in my case 20. We had a similar situation in Germany, but here it's a norm for rich and poor alike.

In the meantime, I settled down in new surroundings. I have prospects, in one or two years' time, of acquiring British nationality for me and my family. Danny, doing very well at school, gave me no reason to doubt his future as an adult. And finally, I've been offered a job where the intensive work, despite some difficulties, should provide me with some joy in the future.'

Chapter 11

The fate of those left behind

At the end of the war, it became apparent that many members of my paternal family had perished. My paternal grandparents perished in 1943 in Sobibór death camp. My father's sister, Margarete Ledermann, her husband, Leo Ledermann, and son Gerhard perished in Auschwitz in 1942. They had been deported there from Amsterdam.

43 Margarete, my father's sister who was gassed in Auschwitz

The fate of those left behind

44 a and b My paternal grandmother Clara and my paternal grandfather Hugo, who were taken by the Nazis from Amsterdam in 1942 and gassed in Sobibór death camp, Poland

45 My cousin Gerhard (Hardie) Ledermann aged 8, March 1936.

46 Gerhard in Amsterdam. He perished in Auschwitz aged 14.

I managed to find out the names of many more relatives who died through translating Hans Sturmann's book, which is dedicated to the members of the Herrmann family who perished at the hands of the Nazis. They are all listed at the beginning of this book (p4-5).

In the end, the vast majority of people in Königsberg and the whole of East Prussia became refugees. By the end of the Second World War, not only was Königsberg bombed by the British, but by the Russians as well. It was literally razed to the ground. Even though my mother's family weren't Jewish, they also had to leave Königsberg once it had been annexed by the Soviet Union in 1945. I think they were just herded out by the Russians. I heard stories of how they walked as I don't think there was any transport. Probably very few of them had cars and if they had cars, they couldn't get any petrol. They all had to travel through Poland to get to Germany.

Uncle Walter and his wife Gretchen, made their way across Germany and eventually ended up in Hamelin. Walter was an architect and he got a job with Hamelin council. In fact, he built his own house there, and he was able to enjoy his favourite hobby as a beekeeper. My parents and I went back to Germany in 1954 to visit Uncle Walter and Gretchen in Hamelin. It was our first trip back after the war. We went by car, which I remember because we had a flat tyre. Hamelin is a quaint city and is best known for the tale of the Pied Piper of Hamelin. It was all very strange because when we met any Germans in the streets, cafés and restaurants, we would think, 'Well, what were you doing during the war?'

We stayed in a hotel, which is where I had my first experience of a duvet. I remember when we came home, we invested in duvets. We were trendsetters! After about a week there, we drove to a town called Darmstadt because my mother had an old friend who lived there. Then we drove on to Switzerland. It was all very strange because it was only 9 or 10 years after the war had ended. We were all glad to get out of Germany and to proper civilisation in Switzerland.

Then in 1964, Uncle Walter came over to see my parents. When Walter and his wife died, they left the house in Hamelin to me, which I sold because I was certainly not going back there.

47 Gretchen Schultz (Walter's wife), June 1944

48 Aunt Gretchen and Uncle Walter, 1946

My mother's older brother, Fritz, was called up and served in the army during the war. He lost his life fighting the Yugoslavian partisans in Yugoslavia. He was killed on 17 May 1944, just a year before the end of the war. He was survived by his wife Elsa and two children, Manfred and Edelgard, who managed to escape to the west together with Elsa's parents. They eventually settled in Southern Germany, not too far from Switzerland. My mother always kept in touch with them and sent presents at Christmas time.

Edelgard married Gerhard Sutter and they had a son called Frank, who I reconnected with about five years ago. Frank has an older sister, Iris, and a younger brother called Volker. Edelgard is now about 77. Elsa passed away aged 95, and Manfred died last year, aged 83.

After they left for England, my mother didn't see her parents, Maria and Ludwig (Lou) Schultz, again.

The fate of those left behind

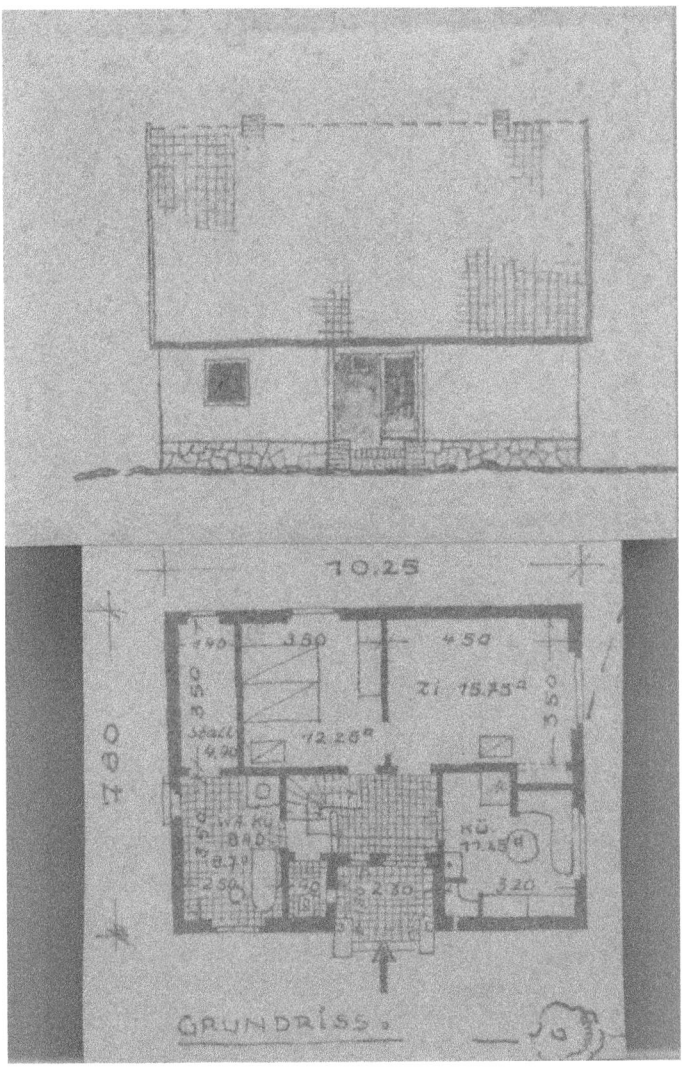

49 Plans of the house and garden Uncle Walter designed and built in Hamelin after the war

50 Uncle Walter and Aunt Gretchen's house, 1951

The fate of those left behind

51 Beekeeper Uncle Walter, 1953

52 Aunt Gretchen in the garden, 1953

53 Walter, Gretchen, my mother and father, 1954

54 My mother, Uncle Walter and Gretchen in Manchester

They were divorced sometime in the late 1930s but, unfortunately, nobody seems to know what happened to them at the end of the Second World War. Both my mother and Elsa attempted to trace them via the Red Cross, but to no avail. They just both mysteriously disappeared.

In my father's letter to Walter in 1946, he talks about the fate of my paternal grandparents during the war, the unknown whereabouts of my maternal grandparents and their divorce.

'Today I finished off a poem that I started three years ago in the summertime. Hopefully, it appeals to you. This poem was written at the time when we still didn't know what had happened to my parents. We were in the middle of passionate struggles with the Italians and although their allies had won many

55 Fritz Schultz, my mother's brother, June 1943

56 Elsa Schultz, Uncle Fritz's wife

The fate of those left behind

57 My cousin Manfred Schultz

58 My cousin Edelgard Schultz

59 Edelgard's confirmation, aged 13 approximately. She is on the front row in the centre.

60 Elsa Schultz, 1965

victories, there was no way to see an end to the conflict. Your report on Opi (Grandpa) Lou is utterly fascinating. It's actually not surprising and inexplicable because perhaps it was going to happen. They had only been living next to each other for many years and, unfortunately, they couldn't often enough defend their mutual dislike of each other. Their love of their two grandchildren somewhat softened and even obscured the situation.

But then we left Germany and shortly afterwards, the war broke out and both sons were conscripted into the army. And so it began for us all, as it did for the parents, a completely changed time, shocking and stressful and under these special circumstances, nothing could be done to bring the two back together. I am beginning to think that fate is most cruel; it has travelled with us, and that makes me feel very sad. Spiritual loneliness is, apparently, still more unbearable than physical pain and torture. We are convinced that you all did as much as possible to prevent the breakup. We know that we, too, could not stop the avalanche.

Brutish people have played recklessly and ruthlessly with the lives of fellow human beings. If those soulless animals had not understood how to betray the trust of stupid people, then perhaps my parents and other members of my family would still be alive, and the meaning of life with my in-laws would not have been so completely destroyed. Nevertheless, I pray to the Almighty that now at last we can soon get some news of Opi Lou and Omi Maria so that with our combined efforts, we can try and shape for them a bearable and happy life for their twilight years.

Chapter 12

School and my Bar Mitzvahs

After moving to Manchester from Liverpool in December 1945, I spent seven months at Old Moat Primary School in Withington where I met Leonard Kaufmann, a fellow survivor. I started at Burnage High School for Boys in September 1946, which was a year early as I wasn't due to take my 11 plus for another year in Liverpool.

At Burnage High, we participated in different sports each term, usually on Wednesdays. We rotated each term between football, rugby and swimming. That is how I learned to play rugby. I must have shown potential playing rugby because when I was in the school office one day, the rugby master asked if I would like to play on the school second under 14 team the following day. And I did quite well. I was fast, so I used to play wing or centre and I rose to team captain very quickly. I remember playing against Manchester Grammar School and we beat them 17-0. I scored all 17 points, five tries and one conversion.

I also used to compete in athletics at school, but I was a late developer in sprinting terms. I managed to make the athletics team by doing the high jump. And I seemed to get faster as I grew older! By the time I got to sixth form, I was representing the school at sprinting. In those days, I used to train only twice a week.

61 Me, aged 10

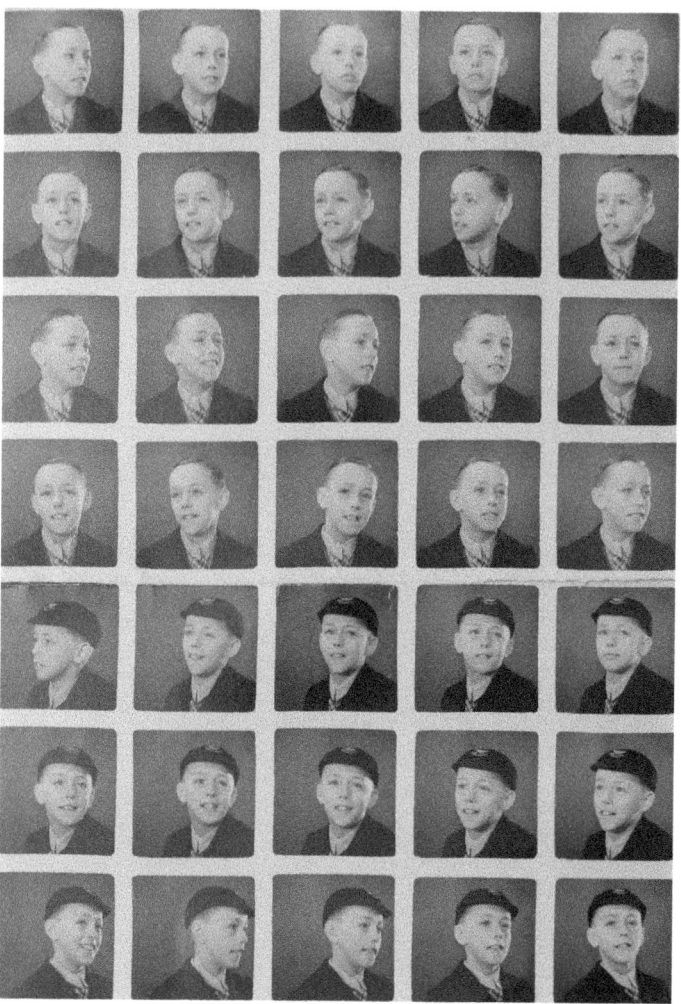

62 Me in Burnage High School uniform, aged 11

School and my Bar Mitzvahs

63 I am standing in the centre on my 11th birthday, 15 September 1946

64 Burnage High School for Boys (I'm on the front row, fourth from the left), 1950

65 Burnage High School for Boys, second under 14s rugby team.
I was captain in 1950.
I am holding the ball.

66 My mother and me, circa 1946/7

School and my Bar Mitzvahs

67 My father and me, September 1948

We weren't particularly religious at home. We kept all the festivals, but we were very much 'middle of the road'. However, when we came to Manchester, we lived about a mile from Wilbraham Road Shul in Fallowfield, in a small semi-detached house. I remember the address, 72 Brentbridge Road, Fallowfield, Manchester 14. One of the first things my parents did was to join the *shul* and they enrolled me in Hebrew classes.

68 Me outside 72 Brentbridge Road, Manchester

Shortly after we joined, the *shul* appointed a new minister, Reverend Felix Carlebach, a fellow refugee from Germany. He subsequently served the congregation for almost 40 years and gained *semicha* early in his career. Sadly, he lost his wife Babette in 1990. She had been his constant loving partner in both family and communal affairs.

School and my Bar Mitzvahs

Reverend Carlebach used to teach the Hebrew classes and called the register every week. He also used to ask whether you went to *shul* on *Shabbat*. By that time, I was at Burnage High and playing in rugby matches on Saturdays. Reverend Carlebach used to say to me, "Why don't you come to *shul* on *Shabbat*?" and I used to make up some excuse. He was very persistent and, in the end, I just told him the truth and said, "Well, actually, I play for the school rugby team." He had no answer to that!

My father and mother only went to *shul* on the High Holy Days and when there was a *Bar Mitzvah* or wedding. I don't know how they felt about religion after the war. They never really spoke about it. I suppose a lot of Jewish refugees were very disillusioned with the whole thing and questioned how religion allowed the Holocaust to happen. But they never really spoke about their feelings.

I had my *Bar Mitzvah* in September 1948 and that is when I first wore long trousers! Mr Goodman taught me my *Torah* portion, which I read at Wilbraham Road Shul. Then we had about 50 people at a Jewish restaurant called the Hadassiah Restaurant, just off Market Street in Manchester. I've still got my father's speech from my *Bar Mitzvah*. We used to get pens for presents and that sort of thing. In those days, it was mainly the parents' friends who were invited, and it was the same with weddings.

I only had two friends from school at my *Bar Mitzvah*. One of my friends was Raymond Goldberg, who lived in Withington and eventually became a doctor. The last I heard of him was that he was a major in the British Army. The other one was Wally Houser, who was a great character and an excellent musician, as was his mother. He played clarinet for the National Youth Orchestra and then became a jazz musician. He played at Ronnie Scott's Jazz Club in London and became a director of the club. He is married and lives in London, and I am still in touch with him. Goldberg and Houser were almost a year older than me because, as mentioned, I was the youngest in my year.

My parents were friendly with Leo Komrower who came over from Germany like the rest of us. When my parents first met Leo, he was living as a lodger with an English family on Mauldeth Road West in Fallowfield, just a few minutes from us. They used to invite him every Friday night for dinner between 1945 and 1960. Leo had a friend called Vonny Hamilton, who was originally from Switzerland. He was also a bachelor who lived as a lodger in Chorlton and we got to know him, so he was also invited on a Friday night. When I was 17 and had learned to drive, I used to go and call for him. They were both older than my father and both retired. Vonny had been a salesman for a photographic company.

I had a second *Bar Mitzvah* in September 2018 at Bowdon Shul when I was 83, which is the usual age to celebrate it. I thought it would be a good idea because I didn't remember much about the first one! I didn't actually say my *Bar Mitzvah* piece, but I got called up and the Rabbi gave a little sermon about it being my second *Bar Mitzvah*. A few friends attended the ceremony, but we didn't have a big party.

School and my Bar Mitzvahs

Mr. Chairman, Reverend Gentleman, Ladies and Gentlemen,
my friends, my dear Danny,

It is with great pleasure that I speak to you a few words on this very happy occasion. Don't be afraid, I shan't bother you with a lengthy speech but I feel I ought to say at least something although practically everything has already been said by more competent and - indeed - eloquent speakers. However much or rather: however little I shall say, I know I would not be able to deminish the brilliancy of their eloquence, however hard I may try.

To come to the point...My wife and I wish to express our sincerest thanks for the most wonderful and really touching manner in which you all proved your sympathetic feeling and your friendly relationship to us not only by taking part in this reception but also on many other occasions in the past. It is reassuring to know there are friends participating fullheartily in pleasant as well as in unpleasant matters, particularly if one has to bewail the loss of almost all close relatives, those dearly beloved ones who would celebrate this day together with us had they not become the victims of a tragic past.

To you, my dear Danny, I want to speak some words, too. This is your special day and believe me, I find it very hard to say in a few sentences what your mother and I feel at the bottom of our hearts on an occasion so significant and important for you. For us it is natural today to pause for a moment and to make a survey of our past which is so full of distress as well as of delight. Years of anxiety and sorrow lie behind us and only a strong will of resistance towards hostile forces has enabled us to again enjoy the comforts of a comparatively easy life - for how long a time we do not know.

My thoughts are today dwelling on the day of my own Barmitzvah. I mentally see my father rising at the festive table amidst the large number of relatives to deliver his speech with great emotion. I shall never forget the deep impression made upon me when he announced that on the occasion of my Barmitzvah his life-long wish had come true and he had made it possible to inaugurate the "Family Herrmann Society" the purpose of which was to cherish the coherence of the numerous relatives and to support any needy member of that society by means of a fund. This has become one of my proudest but at the same time - alas! - saddest memories because that big family has now vanished almost into dissolution. The few survivors or their surviving children live in Eretz Israel now and have started a new life ruled by a far greater idea of the new and promising era of our time. Therefore, because the developments there concern us by no means less than our brethren in Israel, I could not think of any other way of bringing near to you, Danny, our close relation to the Jishuv and their aspirations and at the same time to the way of life of the past, of those who are no more - I could not think of any better way than presenting you yesterday a certificate of the Jewish National

69a My father's speech written on the occasion of my *Bar Mitzvah*, September 1948

Fund for 13 Trees planted in your name in the Forest of Freedom to commemorate the plight of our unfortunate deceased and to have a very small but useful share in the rebuilding of the land of our forefathers. This certificate appears to me an excellent symbolisation of the confluence of the past and the future, and it is in the same light that I see the meaning of this, your day. I know it is the attribute of the growing-up young not to look back – and only rightly so – today – however – not only we, the elder generation turn our eyes back to the past but you too ought to do likewise, if only for a moment, because it is the past alone we are taking our lessons from. And yet, this day provides the ideal platform for an outlook to the future. You know and it has been said before that this day marks the decline of your childhood so sweet and burdenless, and the approaching of your manhood. Your actual life is now taking shape with all its duties and commands, often so difficult but never impossible to bear, coupled with untold pleasures to look forward to. You look out and you will see your future greeting you, a future full of plans, desires and wishes which begin to become more distinct and more concrete with every new day. Your mother and I pray that your future may be a very bright and colourful one reigned by success and achievements at all times. And may this day of your Barmitzvah be the milestone on which in later years when you set out on your journey to an independent life, your roving memories may rest and tell you of the gentle and binding forces of Family and Friendship bonds.

Address delivered at the Hadassiah Restaurant, Manchester, September the 18th, 1948.

69b

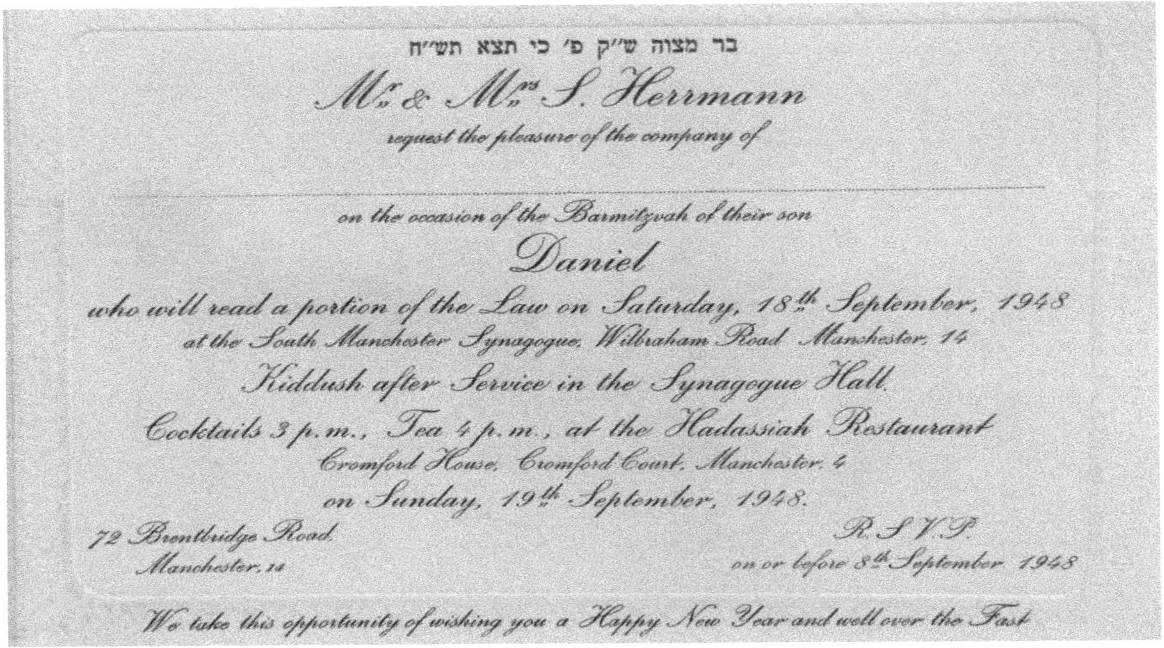

בס"ד אנא ה' הצליחה נא

Mr. & Mrs. S. Herrmann

request the pleasure of the company of

on the occasion of the Barmitzvah of their son

Daniel

who will read a portion of the Law on Saturday, 18th September, 1948
at the South Manchester Synagogue, Wilbraham Road, Manchester 15

Kiddush after Service in the Synagogue Hall

Cocktails 3 p.m., Tea 4 p.m., at the Hadassiah Restaurant
Cranford House, Cranford Court, Manchester 2
on Sunday, 19th September, 1948.

72 Brantridge Road
Manchester 14

R.S.V.P.
on or before 8th September 1948

We take this opportunity of wishing you a Happy New Year and well over the Fast

70 *My Bar Mitzvah invitation, 1948*

71 a and b My 1st and 2nd *Bar Mitzvah* photos

School and my Bar Mitzvahs

72 Family friend Vonny Hamilton, July 1955

Chapter 13

Changing names and naturalisation

In 1949, my father applied for naturalisation and at the same time he changed his name from Herrmann to Herman, with one R and one N, instead of two Rs and two Ns. And he thought he might as well insert an extra name, so he became Siegfried Frederick Herman as his workmates had called him Fred at the factory in Liverpool. My mother went through naturalisation at the same time as my father. He did it for the whole family.

I don't have any other names, but I sometimes used to add an extra name when I was at school. I added in Sydney because that was my foster father's name. I have always been a Danny rather than a Daniel. In Germany they spelled it Dani, with one N and an I. Coincidentally, I've got a cousin called Dani Herrmann, who was a general in the Israeli army. I was once dragged in front of the maths master at school and he said to me, "How DO you spell your name?" This was because every time I wrote my name in school, I spelled it differently, with one R, two Ns, two Rs, one N, and so on, and he wanted to know what it was once and for all! So for my last three years at school, it was Herman with one R and one N, and has been ever since.

My father started his own business called Marsinette in around 1952, manufacturing what was called 'fully fashioned knitwear'. The garments were made on a machine, and nothing was cut by hand. The name Marsinette was derived from 'Mar' - my mother's name Margarete, 'Si' - my father's name Siegfried and 'nette' for terms of payment.

He employed a lady called Janet, who he knew from his time at the Salford knitting factory, to operate the machinery. My father did the designing and supervising. They specialised in manufacturing sweaters and cardigans for golf clubs, and my mother used to travel to golf clubs to sell them. She would go by bus or train, as we didn't have a car then. My father then decided to get some premises on Lever Street in Manchester. However, he was not making enough money, so he closed down the business and became a manufacturer's agent. He was very successful at that.

All of our naturalisation documents were stolen from my father's office workshop on Lever Street, sometime in the 1950s, during a break in. He kept the documents in a small cash box, which was probably stolen, as they thought there was cash in it. My father had put everything in there, including birth certificates and marriage certificates. We would have probably got duplicates, but because we were from East Prussia and it had been taken over by the Russians, it was impossible. I've never been able to provide a birth certificate. All I can show is a letter from the Home Office certifying that my parents had applied for naturalisation and that it was granted.

I only found my mother's passport, which includes me in it, after nearly completing this book. Had I found it earlier, it might have made my life much easier, as far as official forms were concerned. It would have proved my existence and date of birth, rather than having to use the Home Office letter from 1951.

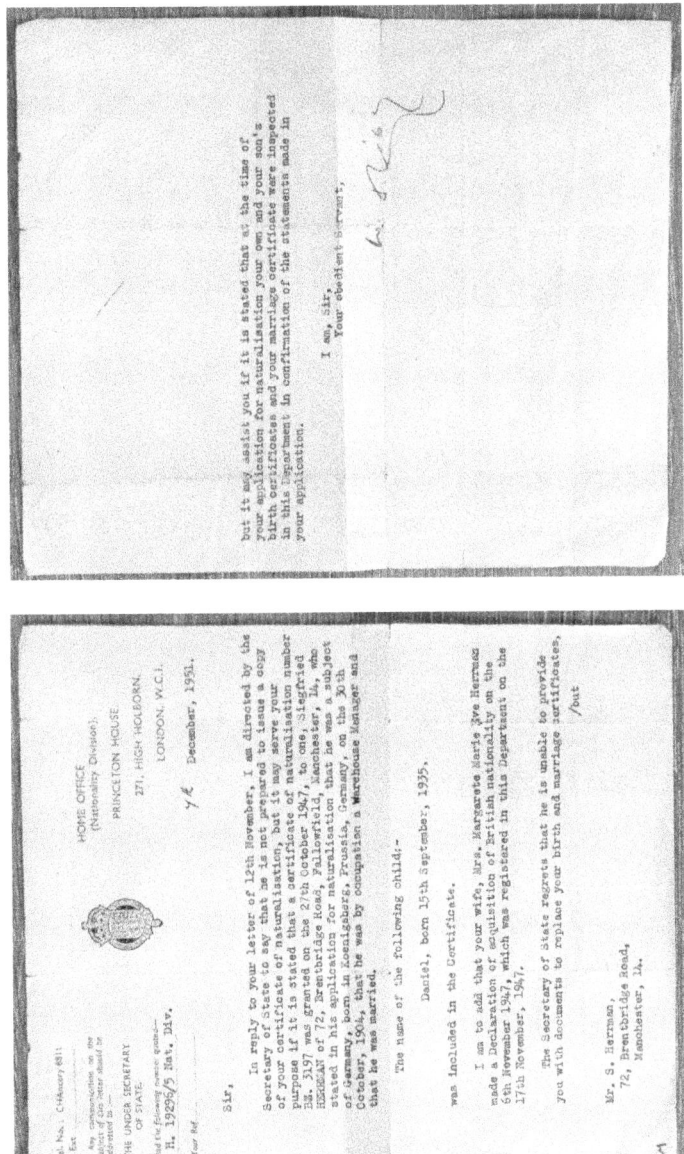

Tel. No.: Chancery 6811
Ext.

Any communication on the
subject of this letter should be
addressed to:—

THE UNDER SECRETARY
OF STATE,

and the following number quoted:—
H. 19296/5 Nat. Div.

Your Ref.

HOME OFFICE
(Nationality Division),
PRINCETON HOUSE,
171, HIGH HOLBORN,
LONDON, W.C.1.

7th December, 1951.

Sir,

In reply to your letter of 12th November, I am directed by the Secretary of State to say that he is not prepared to issue a copy of your certificate of naturalisation, but it may serve your purpose if it is stated that a certificate of naturalisation number BZ. 3197 was granted on the 27th October 1947, to one, Siegfried HERGEAN of 72, Brentbridge Road, Fallowfield, Manchester, 14., who stated in his application for naturalisation that he was a subject of Germany, born in Koenigsberg, Prussia, Germany, on the 30th October, 1904, that he was by occupation a Warehouse Manager and that he was married.

The name of the following child:-

Daniel, born 15th September, 1935.

was included in the Certificate.

I am to add that your wife, Mrs. Margarete Marie Eve Herrmann made a Declaration of acquisition of British nationality on the 6th November 1947, which was registered in this Department on the 17th November, 1947.

The Secretary of State regrets that he is unable to provide you with documents to replace your birth and marriage certificates,

/but

Mr. S. Herrman,
72, Brentbridge Road,
Manchester, 14.

but it may assist you if it is stated that at the time of your application for naturalisation your own and your son's birth certificates and your marriage certificate were inspected in this Department in confirmation of the statements made in your application.

I am, Sir,
Your obedient Servant,

W. Ney

73 a and b Letter confirming my parents' naturalisation, 1951

74 My mother's birthday card from my father, early 1950s

Manches kommt so anders,
Als es mancher denkt,
Ratlos oft Du wanderst
Selten glückbedenkt.
Immer doch wird scheinen
Nach viel Regen Sonne,
Ewig werden auch die Kleinen
Tragen Früchte voller Wonne.
Trüben Kämpfe, stark sei weiter —
Eintracht, Mut, Beständigkeit.

"A very happy Birthday."
Once more I want to say;
And even better, let me wish
A happy Every Day.

With much love
your Siegi

75 The acrostic poem my father wrote for my mother inside the card.
Each line begins with the first letter of his new business name MARSINETTE.

Chapter 14

Meeting Pat

1951 was a special milestone in my life, which coincided with the opening of a new Jewish youth club. The West Didsbury Jewish Youth Club was based at the *Sephardi* synagogue on Queenston Road, using mainly the *shul succah* and the *cheder* classrooms in the neighbouring house owned by the *shul*. It was an instant success and catered for children in the 14 to 18 age group, providing a variety of activities such as guest speakers, dances, table tennis, board games, outdoor sports, dramatics and much more. This venture was the brainchild of the late Barry Wax and Joe Sassoon, who were Chairman and President respectively, along with their group of dedicated volunteers. The majority of the older teenagers were drawn from the major senior schools in the area, namely Manchester High School for Girls, Withington Girls' School, Levenshulme High School for Girls, Manchester Grammar School, William Hulme Grammar School and Burnage Grammar School, Whalley Range High School and a few others.

Meeting Pat

Although Jack Abadi was two years below me at school, I got to know him at the youth club, and together with Danny Betesh, they became two of my best friends. Sadly, Jack passed away in February 2006, and I still miss him very much. Danny and I are still very good friends and meet regularly. I have also kept in touch with Jack Cattan, who married Sylvia in 1959 and has been living in Brooklyn, New York since 1960. In recent years, we have been on holiday together and remain in regular contact.

With no disrespect to Jack Abadi and Danny, the highlight of 1951 for me was meeting Pat at the youth club. It was a case of love at first sight. She was only 14 and still a pupil at Manchester High School for Girls. She was, and still is, very beautiful, tall and blonde, lively and outgoing, fond of most sports, particularly

76 Me, Alex Mizrachi, Jack Abadi, Jack Cattan (crouching) and Danny Betesh

77 Back row (L-R): Syd Sagar, Danny Betesh, Len Gorodkin, Ronnie Brown, me, Jack Saltman, Maurice Hakim
Front row: Lionel Saltman and Johnny Sueke

tennis and netball. But now golf is her favourite, closely followed by bridge.

In the early 1950s, we all used to go out in large groups, whether it be to the cinema or dances organised by local Jewish charities or clubs. Pat was a very popular young lady, and I often had to take second place to many of the young and some older 'beaux' she seemed to favour over me. However, luckily for me and to my great relief, she always came back to me. There were one or two special occasions when we became 'an item' again, such as my 21st birthday and my graduation. In the intervening years, I had one or two other girlfriends, but they were not a patch on Pat and we eventually got engaged in 1958.

Meeting Pat

78 The 'in' crowd at Cottons Hotel, Knutsford, December 1955
Top row (L-R): Raymond Kemp, Sid Sagar, Danny Betesh, Jack Abadi, Jack Cattan, me, Bill Morris, Cyril Harris, Ronnie Brown, Michael Jackson and Henry Cattan
Seated (L-R): Cynthia Lubick, Merle Blaiwais, Loretta Bursk, Pamela Abelson, Pat, Joyce Tawil, Sylvia Tawil and June Stone

I stayed at the youth club for about 18 months, as the only reason for my membership was Pat. Together with most of my male friends, we moved over to South Manchester Maccabi, whose HQ was at Palatine Road opposite the Manchester Country Club. Maccabi catered for the 18 to 30 age group, whereas the Country Club attracted an older and more sophisticated crowd. It boasted much better facilities, such as six tennis courts, a bowling green and had a popular card section, mainly for bridge players. The tennis section had a very talented team, some of whom had played at the Northern Tournament at West Didsbury and even in the early rounds of Wimbledon.

Pat's maiden name was Benster, which her father had changed from Berinstein and Bernstein in the 1930s. Pat's father, Sam, had married her mother, Fay, in December 1930 in Leeds. Their first child, Barbara, was born in October 1932 at home in Prestwich, Manchester. Pat was born in hospital in March 1938 and their third daughter, Valerie, was born at home in May 1941. During his working life, Sam developed a successful textile business in Manchester, from which he retired in 1970.

Prior to and during the Second World War, the family lived in Prestwich, and just after the war ended, they moved to 5 Darley Avenue, West Didsbury. Barbara spent her first year of senior school at Stand Grammar School in Whitefield and then transferred to Whalley Range High School when the family moved to Didsbury. A year later, in 1947, Pat was enrolled at Manchester High School for Girls (MHSG) preparatory department with Valerie. Pat spent one year at Beaver Road Primary School in Didsbury.

Sadly, Valerie passed away very suddenly in March 2011 and not long afterwards, Barbara died in April 2014, aged 81. Whilst Sam died relatively young in 1980, at the age of 76, Fay was only about six weeks short of her 102nd birthday when she died in September 2013. Two years earlier, she'd had the great pleasure of receiving a birthday card from The Queen, congratulating her on reaching her century.

79 Pat, Barbara and Valerie

80 Pat at a fancy dress party in West Didsbury Jewish Youth Club, aged 15

81 Pat wearing a new coat, aged 17

82 Pat (63), Valerie (59), Fay (90) and Barbara (69)

Chapter 15

University and a passion for athletics

I applied to both The University of Manchester and The University of Nottingham and was accepted for both, but I chose Manchester. Back in 1953, university entrance was a completely different system from the present day. The degree I chose was called BA (Com), Bachelor of Arts in Commerce. It was a three-year course which covered a very wide range of subjects, specialising in accountancy, law and economics. There were only about 15 of us on the course and we were all boys. The degree exempted me from the intermediate examination of the ICAEW (The Institute of Chartered Accountants in England and Wales).

I lived at home in Fallowfield, which made it far more manageable for my parents. We were on the number 97 bus route, and the bus stop was about 100 yards from my front door. I would roll out of bed and get on the bus that would drop me off right outside the university! I don't think it was free to go to university then, but you could get a grant from the local authority. I got a bursary, which was based on my A Level results.

At university, I used to participate in a competition called the Christie Championships, which was held every year between Liverpool, Leeds and Manchester Universities, and I was the 100 yards champion. I also took part in the British Universities Championships, which was for all universities in the country. The best I achieved was finishing fifth in the 100 yards final, in 1956.

In my last year at university, I started playing rugby again with my university pals who were from the Isle of Man. We managed to progress through the ranks from about the fifth team to the third team. The university team was of a pretty high standard, so we did quite well to get to third. I played either centre

83 Me, winning the 100 yards race at Christie Championships, Liverpool, 1955

University and a passion for athletics

three-quarters as they called it in those days, or a wing. My friend Jack Abadi was on the team with me, both there and at school.

I left university in 1956, but I continued with athletics at Manchester and District Lads Club Harriers, which later amalgamated with Manchester Athletics Club. I first joined the club in 1946 and I am now the second oldest member, which has entitled me to honorary membership. The club didn't have a proper ground or track - it was a grass track, off Wilbraham Road in Chorlton. However, because I was at The University of Manchester, I paid to become a life member of the Athletics Union, which entitles me to use the university facilities, and I can still use any of their sports facilities today! I competed in many sprint events for my club and became a County and North of England champion.

There was an athletics club called the Mancastrian Club which used to put on international athletics meetings at the White City athletics track and invite top athletes to go there. One year, around 1955 or 1956, Emil Zatopek from Czechoslovakia came with his wife and a chap called Gordon Pirie, who was a top British runner. Zatopek was a fantastic long-distance runner who won the 5,000m, 10,000m and the marathon in the 1952 Olympics. He was called the 'Iron Man'.

On the day that Zatopek was training for the meeting at White City, new tiered steps and seats at the side of the track were being constructed. I saw Zatopek and his wife sign their names in the concrete whilst it was still wet. I have tried to look for them, but it was over

84 My graduation, 1956

University and a passion for athletics

85 Me in Cannes, August 1956

60 years ago and have probably been worn away since. I actually ran in one of those international meetings, in the 100 yards and the relay. I didn't win anything, but it was an achievement to be running in their company, against the top runners of the country.

In 1957, I ran in an indoor meeting at the Kings Hall at Belle Vue, Manchester. It was the first indoor meeting to be held since the war. It was a circular arena, with a traditional circus ring in the middle with seats all around it. The circular track was only about 130 yards, and there was only room for three lanes. It was there that I met Derek Ibbotson, who later that year set a new world record for the outdoor mile. He was competing in the indoor mile at Belle Vue, winning the race comfortably by over a lap. It was initially announced that he had set a new world record for the indoor mile. However, much to his dismay, it was later discovered that the officials had miscounted the total number of laps and he had finished the race one lap short, so the record was invalid.

I also used to run indoors at Cosford RAF station where they held most of the indoor meetings in England at that time. It had a proper 220-yard track.

86 Me competing in the 50 yards indoor race, Belle Vue in Manchester, 1957.
L-R: Reg Cass (UK) in 3rd place, me in 2nd place and Agbaolo (Nigeria) in 1st place.

Chapter 16

The 1957 Maccabiah Games

The Maccabiah Games is a quadrennial, international, Jewish, multi-sport event. In 1957, I applied to take part in the fifth Maccabiah Games. I had to go down to Battersea Park in London to take part in the trials along with my friend Danny Betesh, who was trialling for football and David Caplan, an athlete from Salford. I managed to win the 100 yards, so I was selected to compete in the 1957 Maccabiah Games in Israel for the athletics team. Unfortunately, Danny and David didn't make it.

The games took place in September, which I remember, as I was there for my 22nd birthday. It was my first time in Israel. I was very impressed and overawed by the whole experience. I learned to pace myself in the heat and not overtrain. I finished third in the 100m, fifth in the 200m and was second in the relay, so that was a very good Maccabiah for me.

I didn't have any close friends with me, but I made friends. We had about a dozen people on the athletics team, and you didn't really get to mix with the other teams. However, I remember meeting Ben Helfgott, who survived the concentration camps and became a weightlifter. He is an amazing fellow who, in his later years, received a knighthood in recognition of his work for Holocaust charities and education.

The different sporting competitions were in various venues all over Israel. The opening ceremony was at the Ramat Gan Stadium where about 50,000 people were watching, but the athletics were held at a track just outside Tel Aviv. It really was the lowest grade of track you could have run on, with a temporary stand next to a power station. I remember the very first night we got to the Maccabiah Village, just outside Ramat Gan, it consisted of army tents, with six of us sleeping in each. We had a metal bed, a mattress and an orange box, which was the only bit of furniture at the bedside. You put your case under the bed and that was it! They had proper buildings for the showers and toilets which were about 50 yards away, so if you wanted to go to the toilet at night-time, you had a 50-yard walk or run! There was a proper building for a big dining hall, and the whole village was fenced off.

Nowadays, the Maccabiah has many more sports venues. They have veteran and junior events and it's become more of a sports festival. It was much more difficult to qualify in athletics when I was there. They had heats, semi-finals and finals, whereas now a lot of the events are straight finals, or there might only be two heats and then the final.

Whilst I was in Israel, I met about 20 family members on my father's side who I had not seen before. They lived in a place called Ramot HaShavim, not far from Tel Aviv, which was a *moshav*. They were all chicken farmers and they moved to Israel, which was then Palestine, in around 1936. I met all of them and quite a few were called Herrmann. We have kept in touch ever since, but a lot of them have passed away now. It was nice to have family, as I didn't have many relatives before going to Israel. One of the few relatives I knew in England was my father's second cousin, Charles Singleton, who I called my uncle.

I remember the old grandmother, Gerde, whose husband was a Herrmann and was my father's first cousin. She was widowed by then and was probably in her late 70s, but she seemed to me to be very ancient. She had a hard life looking after the chickens on their chicken farm. Many years after she died, I found out that she had helped my mother to look after me for a couple of years after I was born, before she went to live in Israel.

Gerde had two children, Chavah and Joel. The eldest, Chavah, lived next-door to her and was married to Chanan, with two children, Odi and Michal. When I first went to Israel in 1957, Joel wasn't married, but later he married Yaffa and had two children, Osnat and Arnon. Joel has since died, but Yaffa is still there. Osnat is a top nurse at the biggest hospital in Israel, Tel HaShomer. She is married to Tuvia, a retired policeman.

Arnon is a farmer at the bottom of the Negev Desert, more or less by the Dead Sea, where the temperature is higher than 40 degrees all the time. We went to Arnon's wedding to Galit in Tel Aviv. Galit manages a health spa, which we visited once, and she offered me many treatments. I also went into the Dead Sea, floating, as you do. However, because I've got two artificial knees,

87 Joel and Yaffa's wedding, Israel, circa 1963

88 My father's second cousin, Chavah Vitalis (née Herrmann) with her husband Chanan, children Odi and Michal and my mother, Israel, 1968

I just couldn't get up out of the water, and she had to get two men to lift me up!

I went to *shul* in the *moshav*, which was a makeshift one in the village hall. I hadn't taken a *tallis* with me, so I borrowed one from my relatives and it was so motheaten that if you touched it, it would fall apart. They were not religious people, and they weren't very religious in the *shul* either. At one stage, mine was the only *tallis* in the *shul* and every time someone was called up, they borrowed it and it fell apart again! Most of the members of the *moshav* were immigrants from Germany. They still call people who came from Germany 'yeckers', which means jackets, because the Germans were formal and wore jackets!

I remember, back in 1957, Pat's Israeli relations asked me to bring over some apples, as their children had been prescribed apples for a medical problem. Apparently, there was a shortage of apples in Israel at the time. So when I went to Israel, half of my case was full of apples, and I took coffee in tins as they couldn't get Nescafé then. Nowadays, they have got everything there. I met Pat's cousins at the gates of the village, and I gave them this whole pile of apples and coffee!

Pat and I were not yet engaged, but we were 'walking out' together. Pat's relations spoke Yiddish, which I could understand as it's similar to German, so we were able to make some sort of conversation. I was able to converse in German with my father's family, and they also spoke a little bit of broken English. My parents used to speak German to each other and I could understand them. I did German A level, so I learned all the grammar, but I still needed to practice. When Pat and I got together, Pat used to say, "What did they say?" because sometimes my parents would lapse into speaking German to each other. I would just say, "Oh, they said, we hope City will win on Saturday!"

After the 1957 Maccabiah Games had finished, I took a trip to Eilat in a group of six. One of the guys I went with was called Bert Jacobs. He had a bakery business and was also a keen amateur wrestler who rose to be an international judge. I'm not sure if he was the manager of the British team in the 1957 games or if he went as an official. We flew to Eilat for the day where we visited King Solomon's mines and went snorkelling on the coral reef there, which was fantastic.

Eilat was still being developed at the time and many buildings were under construction. The plane was due to leave at 8pm to go back to Tel Aviv, but when we got to the airport, they said, "Sorry, we made a mistake, we have overbooked. We want six people to volunteer to stay. We will take you back tomorrow morning." We agreed and they put us up in some houses that were just being finished, as the only hotel there was full. The houses had no furniture in them, only beds, and that's where we slept. We ate in the communal dining room with other people, who were probably builders. They gave us some beers and said, "We've got a film on in the village hall tonight, would you like to come? It's in English." So we went to see the film. However, we couldn't hear it, as all the Israelis were cracking peanut shells so loudly! After about half an hour, we walked out and the next morning we got on the plane back to Tel Aviv.

My parents had been to Israel before me when they had met up with one of my father's relatives, Cilli Berkovitch. She was one of the founder members of the Degania Alef Kibbutz in Northern Israel in 1925. I think she lived to be almost 100. She has a son, Eli, who changed his surname to Berkat and was a veterinary surgeon for the Israeli army. He has been to visit us in England.

Chapter 17

A traditional proposal

Pat and I had been seeing each other a little while at the South Manchester Maccabi and the Country Club in Didsbury. In 1956, when she was 18, Pat went to Edge Hill College in Ormskirk to train to be a teacher. I had just finished university.

We got engaged in 1958 but decided not to get married until after I had qualified, so we had a long courtship. I was completing my three-year accountancy training, called articles in those days, at a firm called Radford Edwards & Co, which eventually became part of Touche Ross, a big national firm at the time. It was on Brown Street in the centre of Manchester.

I proposed in the traditional and official way and asked her father first. He gave me a thorough grilling. I was with him for about an hour and as he hadn't said, "Yes" or "No," I said, "Do I take it I have your approval then?" I then arranged to have dinner with Pat at the Bridge Hotel in Prestbury. It was quite a popular place and they had a special dinner dance on a Saturday night for 17 shillings and six pence, which is 87½p in today's money. I was 23 then and had just done one year of my

A traditional proposal

articles. The ring was an emerald cut diamond ring, which I got from a jeweller who was a friend of my parents, a fellow refugee. I knew nothing about rings at all and I had to borrow some money from my father for it.

We had sort of committed ourselves to each other on Valentine's Day 1957 at a friend's birthday party, but we had to delay it a bit because I'd only just started my articles, so we didn't officially get engaged until April 1958 at the dinner dance. We were going to have an engagement party but, unfortunately, Pat's father had a heart attack. Luckily, he survived, but we cancelled the party. Then in September of that year, Pat graduated from Edge Hill College.

I used to go and visit her in Ormskirk. In those days, I had a Vespa scooter and I went a few times on the scooter in winter. There wasn't much to do in Ormskirk other than go to a local restaurant or the cinema, so occasionally we used to go into Southport, which is only 10 miles down the road. We even went there on the Vespa. Pat used to sit on the back, but on a cold winter's day it used to take us the whole of the film just to thaw out! Then my parents lent me their car so we wouldn't get absolutely frozen!

There was one little cinema in Ormskirk and, in those days, the films went on all day. You could go in the middle of a film, watch it to the end and then start again and watch the first part! And that is what we had to do because of the time limit. Pat had a college curfew at 10.30pm. I remember once I wrote a letter, ostensibly coming from Pat's mother saying, 'Please can you give permission for my daughter to stay out a bit longer?'

89 Edge Hill Training College, Ormskirk

We used to like a film called 'High Society' starring Bing Crosby, Frank Sinatra and Grace Kelly. Our song was 'True Love' from that film. In fact, when Pat celebrated her 80th birthday in March 2018, we had a party for her at the golf club and I sang that song, which was very brave of me! I really wanted to play the piano as well and even had lessons. However, that didn't work out, so I had singing lessons instead!

Before we got married, I managed to avoid National Service, which came into force in January 1949 under the National Service Act. Initially, all boys between the ages of 17 to 21 had to do 18 months National Service, and then when the Korean War commenced in 1950, they increased it to two years. When you finished National Service, you were liable to be called up to serve in the Territorial Army (TA), for one or two weeks a year over the next four years. However, you

A traditional proposal

could get a deferment if you were a student or studying for a profession, for which I qualified as I was studying at university. I applied again for a deferment when I started my three-year accountancy training, after my degree. When I got my qualification at the end of the six years, they called me up. By then I was 24.

First, they called me in for a thorough medical and then I had an interview with a sergeant major, who was called a 'careers officer'. He asked me my name and what I wanted to do in civilian life. I said, "I've just qualified as a chartered accountant," to which he replied, "Very good, how would you like the medical corps?" He was either being funny, or he didn't know what a chartered accountant was. A couple of weeks later, in January 1960, I got a letter saying I couldn't be called up for a medical reason. I was told I had bad feet, which was interesting news for 'the fastest Jew in Britain'! I was delighted, as I could continue with my career, and more importantly, get married!

When I qualified in January 1960, Pat and I organised our wedding for 19 June 1960. We got married at Wilbraham Road Shul and Reverend Carlebach conducted the ceremony. We had a reception at what was then the Embassy Rooms in Sale. On the day, the weather was fantastic, a beautiful day with clear blue skies and many degrees warmer than usual.

As my parents' *ketubah* had been stolen from my father's cash box, Pat and I couldn't show it to the *shul*. But Reverend Carlebach had a cousin who had lived in Königsberg and he remembered the family so was able to verify everything. I wore a penguin suit, black tails and a top hat because we got married in the afternoon. Pat wore a long white dress, which had little raised flowers on it, and she looked very beautiful. I was very nervous because I had to make a speech. My parents were delighted because when they were married in 1933 in the synagogue in Königsberg, there was hardly anybody there. They were very proud, and I imagine it must have been very emotional for them!

It was a very big wedding, with over 300 people there. The bridesmaids were Pat's cousins from Leeds and her sister Valerie and my best man was Danny Betesh. Sam Benster, my late father-in-law, said to my parents they could invite whoever they wanted. However, only a few relatives came. They were Charles Singleton and his wife, along with Ellen Rawson, my father's first cousin, her husband Curt Rawson and their daughter Frances. The rest of my parents' guests were just a few friends. Our other relatives had either perished in the camps, or they lived in Israel and didn't come.

Charles acted as a witness at our wedding. He was slightly older than my father and lived in London. His original name was Kurt Sechelsohn, but he joined the Royal Pioneer Corps in the British Army at the beginning of the war and changed it to Charles Singleton, as they said if he ever got captured by the Germans, they would do all sorts of terrible things to him. It was a 'posh' English name, and he always used to come across to me as a formal, serious guy. He had a sad background, as he had lost his first wife and child in the Holocaust. She committed suicide because of the situation in Germany, and his son was taken to a concentration camp. By 1950, Charles was married again to a lady called Annie Lauber, a refugee from Vienna. I am told that they lived happily ever after.

90 Pat and me on our wedding day. Later, our daughter Linda made a *chuppah* out of Pat's wedding dress, which is now exhibited at The Manchester Jewish Museum.

91 Annie and Charles Singleton with my mother

92 Charles Singleton, my mother, my father, Annie Singleton

Chapter 18

Married life

Pat and I went on honeymoon to France and Italy. On our return, we drove to Avignon to get to the airport. I remember it from the song, 'Sur le pont d'Avignon'. There was incessant rain, which meant you could hardly see anything whilst driving, let alone the road markings. Suddenly, there was a curve in the road, and we were pulled over by the police. It turned out that I had gone over the centre line, which I shouldn't have done. I think they just wanted me to pay them a fine, and I made the mistake of giving them my passport. They wouldn't give my passport back to me, so I paid the fine on the spot but in my limited French, I told them it was ridiculous! Just a few minutes behind us was another English couple from Derby who had been pulled over in exactly the same place. We met them when we went to the next town to complain at the police station, but that was a complete waste of time.

We came back on a boat, not a plane, and we got talking to some people. I was wearing a white polo neck sweater and they said, "Do you mind me asking,

Married life

93 On honeymoon, June 1960

94 Pat and me on honeymoon, June 1960

but are you a vicar?" That was the first, and the only time, I have ever been mistaken for a vicar!

Our first home together was number 76 The Avenue, Sale, which was considered to be a very respectable area. I knew it from when I used to play rugby for my school and we had an annual game against Sale Grammar School, which was right at the end of The Avenue. The master used to say to us, "Right, when we walk down The Avenue, we only speak in a low whisper so as not to disturb the residents and walk in double file."

We had some help from my future father-in-law when we bought the house, and we moved in June 1960 when we got back from our honeymoon. It was a double fronted detached house, right at the end of The Avenue. As you went in the main door, the dining

95 Photo from the invitation to our party at 76 The Avenue. L-R: Carl Santhouse, Arleen Santhouse, Pat and me.

room was on the left and the lounge on the right. Behind the dining room was a breakfast room and a morning room with a kitchen at the back of that. We put on a bit of a conservatory behind the lounge, extending the bedroom on top. Together with my father-in-law, we redid the back patio ourselves. He was a bit of a DIY man, and I like to think I was, though most of my efforts fell apart after I built them!

When we first got married, Pat was teaching at Ashton on Mersey School in Sale, and it was very handy because it was about a half mile walk from home. Then she did supply teaching at Sale Grammar School for Girls and then for King David School in North Manchester, which was a bit of a *schlepp* from Sale. We only had one car, a Ford Anglia, which my mother had given to us when we were first married. I can remember its number plate, 1125 NA. I gave it to Pat and then I used to go on the train from Brooklands Station in Sale to Oxford Road in Manchester and from there, I walked to work.

After leaving Radford Edwards & Co, I got a job as a senior audit clerk at a firm called Carter, Chaloner and Kearns, based in a big office block called Canada House on Chepstow Street. It was a similar size to Radford Edwards with four or five partners, and I worked there for a couple of years. Then I went to work for a Jewish firm called Levinson and Franks. At first, they were in a building on Blackfriars Street and after about a year, they moved to Oxford Road, in the same building where there used to be the News Theatre.

News theatres don't exist anymore. In those days, they only showed newsreels, documentaries and cartoons and you would just go in there for an hour or so. If we wanted a night out, we would go to the cinema. We used to love going to the cinema. There was the Odeon, the Gaumont on Oxford Street and a cinema in Withington called the Scala. We didn't go to the theatre much, but we used to go to pantomimes, which were on at the Palace, the Opera House and the Hippodrome. We could also go out in Stockport where there was a cinema and a theatre called the Davenport, which was situated on Stockport Road.

Chapter 19

My business ventures

Just after we got married, I bought a wholesale cigarette, cigar, wine and spirits business. I was still working as an accountant but a friend of ours, Gita, had a business, which was a full-time concern. Her parents had set up the business supplying cigarettes to factory canteens, which they operated from home. They also sold cigars and had a licence for selling wine and spirits. The family were called Koenig, which means king, and the business was given the same name. My parents were friendly with them. Their daughter, Gita, was adopted and had been in a concentration camp. She came over in around 1945 and eventually went to Manchester High School, but she was obviously very, very frail having gone through all that. Gradually, she became stronger, and later got married to a guy called Teddy Buchwald, a university lecturer. Teddy got a position at Sydney University, shortly after they got married.

Gita's parents had died and she ran the business part-time, but it obviously diminished in size. I bought the business from her and was able to operate it from home. Huge vans used to arrive at our house from cigarette companies such as Players and Senior Service. I don't know what the neighbours thought about us unloading these big boxes of cigarettes and *shlepping* them upstairs! We supplied a Jewish-owned company called Trumeter Ltd, in Radcliffe, North Manchester. All these places had canteens and used to order 10,000 cigarettes at a time and sold them on to their staff. These factories started having vending machines and I had to decide whether I was going to install them, but I didn't in the end.

I increased the number of customers and got a few restaurants to buy cigars. Christmas time was busy because people used to give presentation boxes of cigarettes and chocolates to their customers. I also had an ongoing partnership with a company on Lloyd Street. It was quite a big wine and spirits merchant, and we had a joint venture called the Albert Square Tobacco Company. I used to have the contacts for all the obscure brands like Pall Mall and Peter Stuyvesant, and my partner had the wine and spirit connection. In the end, we had the business for about four years. I had got to know a tobacconist near my new office, and he bought the business. It was quite interesting, but I didn't see a future in it really for me, so I stuck with accountancy.

In 1964, I set up my own accountancy practice, Daniel Herman and Co, on Brazennose Street, near Albert Square. I had just one or two clients to start with. Whilst I was building up the practice, I worked with my father for about five or six years to supplement my income. My father was a manufacturer's agent at the time and one of the main firms he represented manufactured plastic baby pants. They don't sell them any more because nappies are disposable now, but in those days, they were worn over cloth nappies. He used to travel all over the country selling these baby pants to wholesalers.

I started travelling as well, once a fortnight, to help him out. I had various areas to visit, including Liverpool. There were about a dozen wholesalers in Liverpool, and it used to take me a day to visit them all. On one of my visits, I also went back to see Lingmell Road in West Derby where we used to live. Baby pants was a bit of a change from accountancy!

During the course of my travels, I went to a wholesaler in Blackpool. It was my first time there and the owner said to me, "Whatever happened to the old Russian Jew that used to come here?" So I said light-heartedly, "That wasn't a Russian Jew, that was my father!" He still gave me an order for 'Ducky', which was the brand name of the baby pants!

In 1967, I joined in partnership with Farrell Leon. We had both worked for Levinson and Franks, and Farrell had set up his own accountancy practice after he left there. We kept in touch and decided to amalgamate our practices on 1 October 1967. We called it Farrell Leon Daniel Herman & Co and moved to premises at 10 Charlotte Street. We stayed there until March 1975, when we bought premises on Wilbraham Road, Fallowfield. It was a large Victorian building spanning about 6,000 square feet, including a cellar. We didn't need that much space, so we kept the ground floor and let the upper floors to Nicky Balcombe Fire Assessors. My parents helped us with the deposit for the property. I think my mother felt that she owned the whole building. She used to bring her friends in to say hello and march, unannounced, into Nicky's premises upstairs!

In 1973, I embarked on another business venture with Farrell Leon, whilst we had the accountancy practice. Sadly, one of my clients had passed away and his widow put his wholesale tool supplier business up for sale. It was quite a substantial business based in Manchester city centre. We ran it for about two years before realising that it could not be successfully combined with an accountancy practice and, fortunately, we were able to sell it. The company owned a three tonne van, and I had occasion to use it for Keith's 6th birthday. Like all boys of his age, he was football crazy, and we invited about 20 of his friends to a party. We then put the 20 boys plus two sets of goal posts in the van, taking them to the nearest playing field where we set up a pitch. Can you imagine that happening today, without the children wearing seat belts?!

In 1988, Farrell and I took on another partner, Alan Cohen, as the practice was growing. When we eventually sold the practice in 1999, Farrell and I left and Alan stayed on. The business still exists as Leon Herman. I was 63 when I retired. In retrospect, I suppose I was quite young to retire at 63 but, with hindsight, it was the right thing to do as we were not really suited to the digital age! Farrell and I keep in regular touch, reminiscing about old times.

Chapter 20

Winning a gold medal at the 1961 Maccabiah Games

By the 1961 Maccabiah Games, Pat and I were married, and she came with me. I arranged for her to stay in Ramat Gan with Hilde, a niece of a friend of ours, Mrs Vogel. She had two children under 10 and lived in a flat, but she managed to put Pat up, which was very kind of her. For me, it was back to the tent system again. We had been upgraded to a purpose built dormitory, sleeping 25 to a room, but it was so hot that six of us opted to go back to a tent!

We used to have card passes, which I managed to forge because Pat wasn't allowed to come into the Maccabiah Village. I used to put my tracksuit on, run out and say to the guard on the gate that I was going for a training jog. I then met Pat outside around the corner somewhere, and she put my tracksuit on. I came back without a tracksuit, just my shorts and vest, and she showed the pass. That's how I got her in! We used to get invited to many events during the games, and Pat managed to come with me to all of them. On one occasion, the whole British team was invited to the ambassador's residence, which

Winning a gold medal at the 1961 Maccabiah Games

was a very nice villa in Herzliya, for afternoon tea. We had a conversation with some of the embassy staff there, who told us how much they enjoyed working in Israel because they had to observe all the Christian, Jewish and Muslim holidays, which left very little time to work!

We won a gold medal at the 1961 Maccabiah Games, on the same rotten old track. We had a very good guy on the team called Dave Segal, who was a full British international athlete. In the previous Olympics in 1960, he got to the semi-final of the 200m, but then he made two false starts so he was disqualified. My claim to fame was that I beat him a couple of times in the 100 yards in the Highland Games in Edinburgh and a Maccabiah trial at Brighton.

The relay team consisted of Dave Segal, Roger Bruck, Alan Abrahams and me. Roger is a very good friend of mine whom I got to know at the Games. I have been friendly with him, through athletics, ever since, and he lives in London. When it came to the 4 x 100m relay, Alan started off, Roger was second, Dave was third and he handed over to me. It was touch and go with an American athlete, but I managed to hold him off, as I had beaten him once before. It was a fantastic feeling to have won the gold medal in the Maccabiah. It still occupies pride of place in my home.

I remember how seriously makeshift travelling was, at times. Somehow, Dave and I got detached from the main party, and we missed the bus taking us back to the village. We had no money and were dressed in just a vest, shorts and spiked shoes. We had to walk to find the nearest bus and plead with the driver to be allowed on for free. He was happy to give us a free ride when we showed him our gold medals!

When we had free time after the games, we used to visit our relatives. My cousin Joel arranged a party and invited the whole family. I remember one day he took me in his jeep to visit an Arab worker. We sat down on the floor in his hut, and he served us tea and fruit, and then we went to a café in the Arab village where we had very strong coffee.

I also visited a relative, Hermann Sluszewer, who was one of my father's many cousins. He was the son of Bertha Herrmann, who was the sister of my grandfather Hugo Herrmann and had been in Israel since the 1930s. He was born in 1893 and died in 1967. He was an eminent gynaecologist, and he lived on a very fashionable street in Tel Aviv called Rothschild Boulevard, which had an elegant lines of trees. When I first met him in 1957, he was a doctor for the Maccabiah Games.

We also visited Pat's relatives at their *kibbutz*, the ones we gave the apples to. There had been a tragedy in the family. One of the sisters, Rivka, was married to Yossi who drove for Egged bus company. One day, they went on a trip from their *kibbutz* and were ambushed in broad daylight on the main road, just outside Tel Aviv, near what was called the Country Club. It was one of the first terrorist attacks and the bus was shot up. Sadly, Rivka and their two children were killed in this attack, and Yossi lost both his legs. He recovered and became quite famous touring around Israel, giving inspirational talks to people who had been injured in war and to victims of terrorist attacks.

Winning a gold medal at the 1961 Maccabiah Games

96 The winning GB 4 x 100m relay team at 1961 Maccabiah Games.
Back row: Dave Segal Middle row L-R: Monty Samuels (manager), me, Alf Wilkins (coach)
Bottom row L-R: Roger Bruck, Alan Abrahams

97 Me wearing sunglasses, receiving the baton from Dave Segal on the final leg of the 4 x 100m relay at the 1961 Maccabiah Games. Taking over on the final leg for the USA was Mike Herman (no relation), with Israel in the middle and me on the inside for GB.

The final order was GB 1st, USA 2nd and Israel 3rd.

98 My first gold medal for the 4 x 100m relay from the 6th Maccabiah Games, 1961

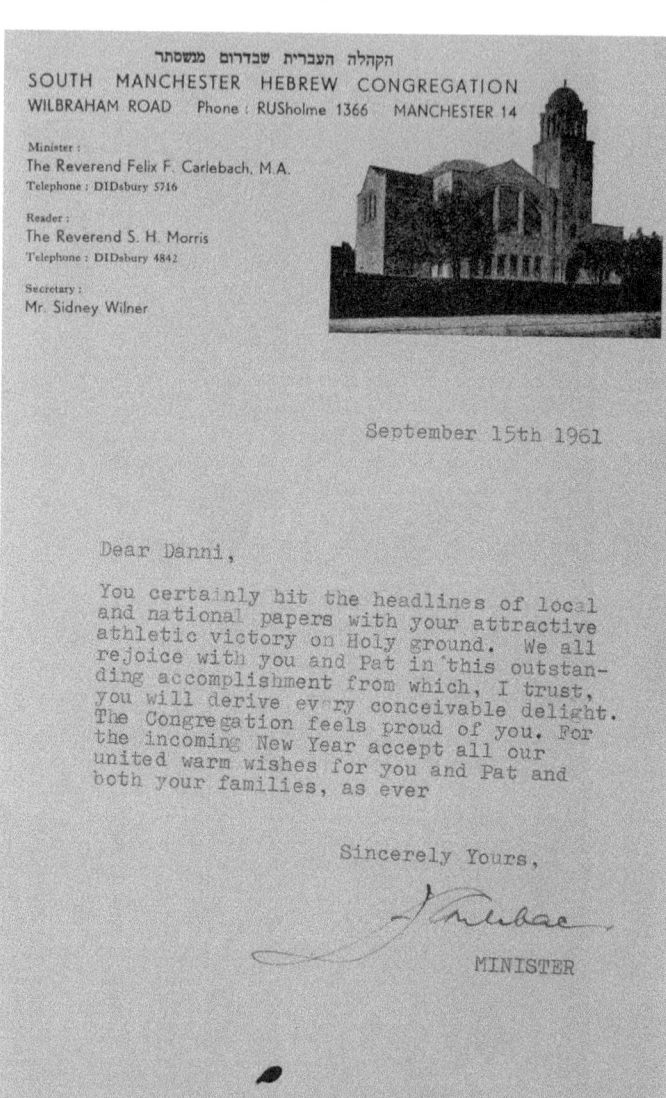

99 Letter from *shul* minister, Reverand Felix Carlebach congratulating me on my sporting achievements, 1961

Chapter 21

Our children

Our first child, Linda, arrived on 17 February 1963, which I always remember! In those days, you used to get a tax allowance for having children and I had to enter the name of the child and her date of birth on my tax return. In my accountancy practice, in about nine cases out of ten, my male clients did not know the birth dates, and they would say, "I'll have to ring my wife." But I always knew my children's birth dates.

Pat went into labour with Linda when we were on our way to a 21st birthday party of one of my athletics friends. Linda was born in Southfields Maternity Hospital, a big old Victorian house in Bowdon. I always remember it was a terribly cold winter. About two or three weeks before Linda was born, I decided to run in an indoor athletics meeting in a place called RAF Feltwell. It was on the other side of the country, near Norwich, and the meeting was held on probably the coldest day of the year. A few other athletes and I set out at 6 o'clock in the morning and experienced every sort of weather: sleet, snow, ice and fog. It took us six hours to get there, and we had about an hour to stretch our legs and loosen up before it started. Then at 6 pm, we left again and got home for midnight.

My coach's wife, Carol Bailey, was a former international sprinter and was also pregnant at the same time. She stayed with Pat while we were careering off to Feltwell! In those days, there were no mobile phones, so you couldn't keep in touch; you just hoped for the best. It worked out in the end and, as it happens, I ran the best time I ever did indoors. I ran in 6.3 seconds for an indoor 60 yards race, which equalled the best time achieved by anyone that year.

Just before Karen was born, we employed our first au pair, Barbro, who was 18 and came from Sweden. She was a very intelligent girl and got a job working as a receptionist with one of the airlines at Manchester Airport. Her family had a factory manufacturing rainwear and were friends with Sven-Göran Eriksson, the former England football manager. She is 75 now, and we have always kept in touch. We have seen her a few times over the years, including at our golden wedding party in 2010. After Barbro, we had a succession of au pairs because Pat went back to teaching between having the children.

Karen was born on 28 February 1964, also at Southfields. There is only one year and two weeks between her and Linda. Then Keith was born on 27 April 1967 at Wythenshawe Hospital. Pat and Keith then went to Southfields and he had his *bris* there.

Julie was born on 10 April 1971 also at Wythenshawe and hers was the first birth I actually attended. It was on the first night of *Pesach*. My late father-in-law used

Our children

to always have *seders* at his house with a black tie dress code, so I went to the hospital in a dinner jacket! It was unusually hot inside the theatre and they let me take off my dinner jacket. I was terrified when Julie eventually appeared, and I thought the doctor was going to drop her! I was no use at all at the birth and afterwards I went back to the *seder*!

All the births were normal deliveries. Pat was an expert!

After all our children were born, we decided to extend the house. We joined the morning room to the conservatory across the back of the house, and I designed an extra bathroom. There were two bedrooms on one side of the house and I made a bathroom in between them. It helped because there were six of us in the house. Then we had a loft conversion to create a room on top, which eventually Karen moved into.

We had a few incidents with Keith over the years. In 1970, we went on holiday to the Scilly Isles, off Penzance in Cornwall, with the three older children and the Harris and Solomon families. There were about 16 of us all together. We more or less took up all the places on the helicopter to the Scilly Isles. We stayed in the only hotel there, which had a swimming pool. We were all at the pool one day when one of the old ladies who was sitting by the pool knitting said, "Is there someone in the water down there?" It turned out to be Keith at the bottom! Gordon Harris was the nearest at the time and pulled him up by his hair. Luckily, Keith was fine.

There was another incident on that holiday when we all went out walking. We had to stand to one side whilst walking up a hill on a narrow road because there was a Land Rover coming up the road. There was a big Alsatian dog running with the Land Rover. Keith took one look at the dog and ran forward into the side of the Land Rover. Fortunately, the car stopped immediately. Keith banged his head and ended up with his feet underneath the car and his head between the two wheels. It turned out the driver was the only doctor on the island, so he picked Keith up, who was momentarily concussed, and drove us to the hospital where they checked him over. Keith has had an aversion to dogs ever since, including Julie and Damian's lovely dog, Bailey! However he has made an exception for his own beloved dog, Chloe!

When I was away for two weeks without the family at the 1973 Maccabiah Games, there was another incident at home with Keith. He was six at the time, and we were living in Sale. Pat could smell something burning, which seemed to be coming from Keith's room. She went to Keith's room and saw smoke and flames. He was between the twin beds reading and there were flames on the bed behind him! He had been fiddling about with matches. Pat went to the nappy bucket and threw all the water out of it over the flames to douse them, but the bed was still smoking, so she phoned our neighbour, Barrie Bernstein, who lived a couple of houses from us. He came round and immediately opened the window and threw the whole bed out of it. Fortunately, the window was big enough to do it, just about!

100 Karen and Linda, aged 2 and 3

101 Our sporting family at Manchester Jewish Sports Meeting, Stretford, 1970
Back row: Linda Herman (now Price), Pat, me and Robert Whiteson
Middle row: Kenny Wax, Karen Herman (now Wright) and Keith Herman
Front row: Derek Wax, Debbie Wax (now Alkalay) and Stephen Whiteson

102 Pat and me with our children
L-R: Karen (11), Julie (4), Linda (12), Keith (8)

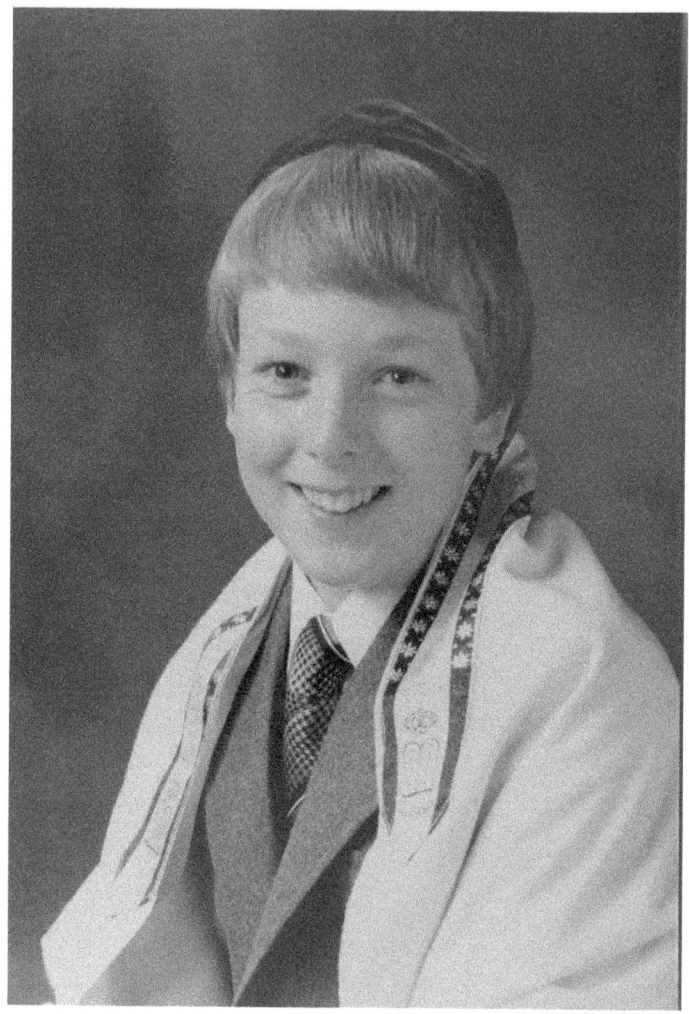

103 Keith at his *Bar Mitzvah*, April 1980

104 Our extended family at Keith's *Bar Mitzvah*

Chapter 22

Finding time for my athletic activities

Pat was very, very tolerant of my running. I remember two weeks before we got married, I told my mother I was going to Liverpool for the Lancashire championships. My mother replied, "You can't go there, as you're getting married in two weeks' time." I said I wouldn't go, but on the day, I packed my bag and threw it out of the window into the garden. Then, when she wasn't watching, I sneaked out and put it in the boot of the car! I told her I was going to see Pat and drove off to Liverpool. I still ran in those championships and came third in the 100 metres.

They had some good runners in Lancashire at the time. There was a guy called Alf Meakin who was an international runner for Great Britain. In August 1957, I ran against him in a handicap race at Chester Racecourse, the day before I went to Israel for the Maccabiah. It was an unusual race because it was a 220-yard straight, so rather than running around the track, you ran in a straight line, which makes it very difficult to judge your pace. Alf won of course and I came second. I remember back to 1953 in my very first handicap race at St Mary's Playing Field in Prestwich, I was given an 8-yard start in the 100 and a 16-yard start in the 220. I won them both quite easily.

Pat didn't always go with me to the local meetings. We always joke about the fact that she went with me to places like Israel, Spain, France or somewhere exotic, but not to places like Wigan or Barnsley!

The Highland Games is quite a prestigious event, which used to take place during the Edinburgh Festival. It was held at Murrayfield Stadium because, in those days, they didn't have a proper track in Edinburgh, so they marked a track out on the rugby pitch. It was a 100-yard straight, but it wasn't big enough for a 440-yard track. Besides the regular athletic events, they used to have traditional Scottish events at the Highland Games, such as Scottish country dancing, tossing the caber and throwing the weight for height. There were all these big Scottish men wearing kilts and performing. There were a lot of invitation events for top runners from all over the world, including the intercity relay, which was a medley relay, 352 yards round. Two sprinters ran half laps of 176 yards each, the third runner ran one full lap of 352 yards and the final, middle distance runner completed two full laps of 704 yards.

The medley relay was always between the same cities: Manchester, Birmingham, Glasgow, Edinburgh and Belfast. It was either us or Birmingham who won because Birmingham had international runners, and we also had some very good runners on our team. I always did half a lap and managed to qualify for the team every year. They used to put us up in a bed and breakfast run by an Irish landlady who gave us fantastic food. We would drive up on a Friday, which took about six hours, and there was a banquet at the Town Hall on Saturday night for all international and intercity competitors. Then we would go and watch the Highland Military Tattoo. It was a great weekend!

One year when we drove up, one of our team managed to drive his car into a field. The farmers wouldn't pull him out until he paid them something! That was the same year that Pat's sister Valerie got married and I got into real trouble because I should have been there for the *aufruf* on the Saturday. However, I was running in the Highland Games! I came, literally flew back early, and made it in time for the wedding on the Sunday!

In early September 1964, there was an athletics meeting to mark the opening of the newly laid track at Longford Park, Stretford, and they invited many of the potential British Olympic runners. The Games that year were held in October in Tokyo, and they used some of the events at Longford Park as trials. I ran and finished fifth in the 100 metres. Ron Jones, who was an athlete in three consecutive Olympic Games from 1960, won it. Lynn Davies also ran and ended up winning Gold in the long jump in Tokyo.

In 1965, my in-laws, Fay and Sam Benster, came with us to the Maccabiah Games and we took Linda. We had relatives on a *kibbutz* not far from Safed, so we

Finding time for my athletic activities

went up there to visit them. Sadly, they have since passed away. By then, things had improved for the Maccabiah Games, as they had a bit more money. Pat stayed with her parents and Linda in a hotel, but I still had to stay at the athletes' hotel. I had the honour of captaining the team. By then, I was probably the oldest on the athletics team.

We saw lots of changes in Israel and everything appeared smarter. They had built new roads which were properly paved, not just dirt tracks. My father's best friend in Germany, Bruno Sandelovsky had emigrated to Israel. He lived in a place called Magshimim, which was a *moshav* not far from the airport, and he had a son and a daughter, Yoram and Nurit. In 1957, Yoram had finished his army service and started university. I remember he came to see me the very first night I arrived. He rode a bike while holding another bike! I don't know how he managed it through the rough tracks with no lighting, but he made it to me so I could ride this second bike back to his place. It was quite frightening really because we couldn't see a thing and they were rough tracks. Anyway, I'm here to tell the tale! I remember when we were there in 1965, Pat, Linda and I went to see them again.

In March 1965, I got my full international vest running for Great Britain after I finished third in the 60 yards in the British Indoor Championships in Cosford. It was so close. I ran the race in 6.5 seconds, and the winner did it in 6.3 seconds! 1965 was probably my best season because I did well in quite a few indoor meetings.

105 1964 Olympic trials at Stretford
L-R: unknown, me (19), Barry Kelly, Ron Jones, Mel Cheskin and Lynn Davies

106 Me winning an indoor race at Cosford, 1965

107 My trophy for the 60-yard sprint for GB against USA, Wembley 1965

Chapter 23

The European Maccabi Games

The European Maccabi Games are held every four years, in between the Maccabiah Games. They are essentially for Jewish athletes to compete from European countries plus Israel. The first one I tried for was the 1959 games, which were being held in Copenhagen. They held trials in Brighton, and I had taken my final chartered accountancy exams seven days before the trials. I had been studying, so had done no training for six months. I thought I had better just take part in one race beforehand, so I ran a race in Manchester a few days before the trials. The day after, I was as stiff as a board, but I managed to loosen up a bit before the weekend. However, I couldn't run at all on the day and I didn't even qualify. Pat also took part in the trials but failed to qualify in the discus event in which she finished second.

I competed in the 1963 European Maccabi Games in Lyon, France. We only had Linda then and we left her at home with my mother. Pat and I went to the games, which were held over a weekend. When we got to the track, they said, "Does anybody here speak French?"

Pat said she did, and they asked if she would like to be the announcer, so she made the announcements in French and in English!

Great Britain had a very strong entry in nearly every event, with a team comprising 20 athletes in all. The Israelis also had a strong team. When it came to the sprints, my friend Roger Bruck won the 100m, with me coming second. Then the order was reversed in the 200m which I won, with Roger coming second. Unbelievably, we are still the holders of those championships because, since 1963, the athletics events have never been held again. This is because only Great Britain and Israel have been able to raise an athletics team during the last 59 years!

In 1993, the European Maccabi Games were held in Antwerp, where Pat made her debut! She was asked to play on the golf team and at the same time, Keith was on the Futsal team, similar to five-a-side football. The only problem was the golf was held at a golf club 15 miles to the south of Antwerp and the Futsal was being staged at a stadium 10 miles to the north. I had to hire a car to drive between the two places to support and watch my family competing.

Chapter 24

My involvement with Manchester City

I have been a City Blue since I was a child, as when I moved to Manchester in 1945, we lived only a mile away from the ground. Naturally, all the local kids supported City and they soon persuaded me to follow suit. However, my real involvement with Manchester City Football Club started in 1967 through my friend Joe Lancaster, who was a former world record holder for running 20 miles and had become a sports journalist. He set up a freelance sports agency and knew the chief football correspondent for the 'Daily Express', Bill Fryer. Bill knew City's manager, Joe Mercer, and the assistant, Malcolm Allison.

One day, in about August or September 1967, Bill suggested to Joe Mercer that the squad should try athletic training and said he would introduce him to Joe Lancaster. They met and City were interested, so they asked for a demonstration session at Maine Road. Joe got me to do the sprints because by that time, I had been an international athlete and was probably one of the top sprinters in the area, but I was getting past my sell-by date! He also asked Derek Ibbotson, the former world mile record holder, who was also getting past his best!

I was delighted to go along to Maine Road. We put the squad through their paces, including a series of sprints, and they liked the idea, so we arranged to do a six-week series of sessions. We started on the following Monday. By then, I was partner in a local accountancy practice, so I could take off the time to do it. I drove to Maine Road and went in through the players' entrance into the dressing room, which was a dream!

In those days, it was pretty basic and nothing like the dressing room they've got today. It was just a big square room and all the first and second team were there, so there would have been about 25 to 30 of them. We all changed, piled into our cars and drove to Wythenshawe Park to start our training session on the red shale track.

The routine was that we did a few warming up stretches with Joe and then we went for a long run, circuiting the park, which was about two miles. Then it was back onto the track for the endurance and sprint workouts. I got to know all the players at that time, which was October 1967. We completed the first six weeks and it all went well, including the City team results, so we carried on. We did it more or less throughout the whole season and that was the year they won the First Division Championship. They had just got back up to the First Division in the previous season. At only their second season back, they won the league, and in their third season, they won the FA Cup.

The players had been fit from the start, but it was a different type of fitness. It was quite hard for me though as I used to play football for South Manchester Maccabi on a Sunday morning and then do the sprint training with City on the Monday morning. I could probably beat all the players at the 100m, although some were very quick off the mark, especially Francis Lee. Colin Bell would have made a very good 800m runner. I think Tony Book, who I'm still friendly with, was one of the fastest, even though he was a full back.

We were training with them in 1969 for the FA Cup Final against Leicester. They hired a train for all the City staff and entourage, and we were invited to go on with our wives. There were about 400 people on the train and the champagne was flowing; no expense was spared in those days! The train stopped at Watford, and we all transferred to coaches to take us to stay at the Waldorf Hotel. Pat and I were at the front on the first bus, and so we went down Wembley Way waving to everybody!

We were of course given tickets to the match, which City won 1-0. The evening after the match, it was customary for the winners to go to the Café Royal, just off Piccadilly. They had a celebration banquet, and they recorded Match of the Day from there. Not all of the 400 people were there, but we were fortunate enough to be invited. I've still got a magnum bottle of champagne as a souvenir, though it's an empty bottle now! The next day, we came back again on a private train with everyone including the players, and we were transferred to buses from Wilmslow to Manchester.

The players went around the town on a double decker open top bus, and we were in the bus behind. Then there were speeches at the Town Hall. It was a great occasion!

In 1970, City won the League Cup. We were still training with them, so once again we went down on the train and stayed at a hotel. They didn't have a banquet that time but had a dinner at a different London hotel and Pat and I were invited.

City played in the European Cup Winners' Cup in 1970 because they had won the FA cup the year before. They got to the final and played a Polish team called Gornik, in Vienna. We weren't invited on the official City bus then, but we went on a three-day trip and saw the match. At the match, there were only around 10,000 spectators, about 8,000 from City, 200 from Poland and the rest were locals. So they announced that everyone should move down to sit in the middle of the stands, which we did. It was a very nice stadium but completely open, and it started raining at half-time. It was terrible and we got absolutely soaked. In fact, it was a wonder the game wasn't called off! City managed to win 1-0, and afterwards we went back to our very ordinary hotel, to get dried off. We went to have a meal at the hotel where the players were staying and ended up in the same room as them. Then half-way through, the waiter came up with a bottle of champagne and said, "With the compliments of Mr Allison!"

We like to think we made a small contribution to City winning the four trophies during the time we trained together. Some of the London teams started doing that sort of training and now it's how most teams train, but it was very new then. We finally finished training with them in 1972. We did a couple of private sessions out of season, and I remember later Dennis Tueart came along. I got to know him quite well. On a Tuesday and Thursday night, we used to sprint out on the grass in the middle of Mauldeth Road West, where it meets Withington Road, on the Chorlton side. In those days, if the grass was too soft and soggy, we used to train on the pavement. When you think about the facilities they have got now, the players wouldn't dream of going out on the public highway to train!

Malcolm Allison left Manchester City in 1972 and went to Crystal Palace, but then he came back to City in 1980. I did one or two more sessions with City. We had a few guest appearances at the sessions from Jonah Barrington, who was a world squash champion, and also from a Coronation Street star and a boxer. However, it fizzled out as it was getting hard for me because I was 45 by then. Although I was probably at my peak as a veteran, I was still trying to lead the training and do what the players did, but it became harder and harder.

108 Me training Manchester City players at Wythenshawe Park running track, 1970
L-R: Derek Ibbotson, Freddie Hill, me, Glyn Pardoe, Wyn Davies, Francis Lee, Arthur Mann, Alan Oakes, Mike Doyle, Mike Summerbee

109 Me training with Manchester City at Wythenshawe Park in 1970
L-R: Mike Summerbee, Tony Book, Mike Doyle, Francis Lee, Freddie Hill, Wyn Davies, me, Colin Bell, Alan Oakes, Derek Ibbotson, Tony Towers, Malcolm Allison

110 Malcolm Allison and me, training in Wythenshawe with Manchester City, 1970

Chapter 25

Memories of the children growing up with my parents

My parents loved it when I got married and had children. They were very much involved, which was lovely. My mother was responsible for them all learning to swim and would take them to Wythenshawe baths to teach them. She helped Pat in the kitchen and she used to cook for us. Everything she cooked was very good. She used to make a famous dish that originates from Königsberg, called *Königsberger Klopse*. It's a meatball that is boiled in an onion based sauce which becomes sweet and sour, and she taught Pat how to do it. She also used to make a marble cake and an *apfeltorte*, which was cake with apple slices on top.

One year, my parents took the kids on holiday to Mallorca without us because it wasn't easy financially for us, with four children. They took just Linda, Karen and Keith, for two weeks to Palma Nova. However, we were feeling a bit sorry for ourselves, so we booked the second week without telling them. We arrived at the hotel with Julie, who was about two or three. We went to the corridor near their room and asked Julie, who could walk and talk a bit then, to go and knock on their door. My father opened the door and said, "*Oma*, there's a kid here that looks just like Julie!" It was so silly, but it was a lovely surprise for them!

My mother took the children everywhere. She used to take them to school and helped all of them when they were a bit older. When their friends were studying German, she used to help them with their German homework and give them lessons. The funny thing is I didn't recognise my parents' accent and didn't think they had strong accents, but the kids recognised it. My mother used to refer to Wythenshawe Park as 'Vyzensher Park'. And when people used to ask her, "Where are you from?" she used to say "Scotland!"

My mother was very generous. Pat used to order from the greengrocer in those days, and *Oma* used to pick up the groceries and then the kids from school. Pat used to ask, "How much is it?" but my mother would say, "No, no, no." Pat insisted we paid, but she could see *Oma* was really disappointed. This happened for a few weeks and then my mother stopped offering to pay. Pat realised afterwards, when she did the same for our children, how much it must have disappointed my mother because that was something that she could have given to us, and we hadn't let her because we were proud. We tell our children this story and say, "If we offer to pay for something or offer to do something for you, say, 'Yes please' because it's not for you, it's for us really."

My mother did an O-Level in English. She started it in 1978, the year before my father died of cancer. She didn't want to carry on after he died, but we persuaded her to, and she passed with a 'C' at the age of 69. Her teacher complained that she was better than that, and they regraded it to a 'B'!

My parents had moved in 1962 from the house on Brentbridge Road to 33 Netherwood Road, Northenden, where my mother continued to live for a few years after my father passed away. She then moved to a retirement flat in Altrincham, called Easingwold. It was at the top of Regent Road.

111 My parents in Cala Blanca in Mallorca, 1976

113 Mother sitting on the far right with friends in the grounds of Easingwold, Altrincham, 1996

112 33 Netherwood Road

114 Mother at Karen's graduation, 1986

Chapter 26

My veteran athletic career and The Foxtrotters

I started a new career as a veteran athlete in 1976, and I ran in my first European Veteran Championships in 1978. From 1978 to 2000, I trained with a group of runners, led by a very good athlete in his day, Brian Fox. We eventually called the group 'The Foxtrotters'. Brian was a similar age to me. He was a runner and a physiotherapist. We had three venues, one being Styal Woods, where we used to run through the woods, warm up and then go back into the woods, run down by the river and sprint up the paths. Afterwards, I always used to lie down on a bench at the top of the hill to recover. When I finally decided to call it a day, 'The Foxtrotters' presented me with my own miniature bench, with a plaque saying 'Danny's Bench' on it. I still keep it on the windowsill in a prominent place of honour. We also ran from Wilmslow to Quarry Bank Mill and back as a warm up, and then did repetition sprint sessions on the pitch and putt golf course. The other venue we used was Alderley Edge.

There were about 30 athletes in the group such as Andy Carter, Alan Mottershead, Norene Napier (née Braithwaite) and Sandra Dyson. Membership of the group was not limited to athletes, and 10 to 15 of us usually ran at any one time. One was an international trampolinist and another was ranked Britain's third women's tennis player, Mandy Grunfeld. In 1991, Mandy played Martina Navratilova in the third round of Wimbledon and won four games. She was an old girlfriend of Keith's. Keith fancied himself at tennis, so he challenged her to a match, and she absolutely wiped the floor with him! Robbie Brightwell and his wife Ann Packer even joined us once. Their sons, David and Ian Brightwell, played for Manchester City.

In 1980, I won the British Masters 100m Championship when I ran the 100m in 11.8 seconds, which wasn't bad for a 45-year-old! My best achievement as a veteran was finishing third with bronze medals in the 100m, 400m and 4 x 100m relay in the 45 to 50 age group, in the World Veteran Athletic Championships in Christchurch, New Zealand, in 1981. I also came fourth place in the 200m final there. I discovered about three years later that the South African who finished second in the 100m and the 200m should have been disqualified for running in the wrong age group. He had overstated his age and should have run in the 40 to 45 grade. That would have promoted me to silver in those races. Nothing was ever done about it, but at least I have the satisfaction of knowing that at one small period in my life, I was the second fastest Jew in the world aged 45! Another interesting statistic from those games is that in the 200m final (45-50) five of the eight finalists were Jewish! One Australian, one Brit, one American, one South African and one Israeli.

I entered the Spanish Masters Championships in 1992, the same year that the Olympic Games were held in Barcelona. The Veteran Championships were held in Jerez, where the sherry comes from, so we flew to Seville and travelled down to Jerez. The games were held over two days in June, and I won the 100m, making me a Spanish champion! I was allowed to run as a guest, but they couldn't actually call me the Spanish champion, so the Spanish guy who came second was called the champion! Then I came second in the 200m. Normally you don't get prizes, just medals, but I got my medal and a bottle of sherry - in fact, everybody got the sherry!

Having won the 100m in Jerez, I turned out to be the first Englishman to win a gold medal over 100m that year, and the second was Linford Christie! I didn't know Linford Christie, but I did know quite a few of the international athletes who were more my contemporaries, such as Ron Hill, who was Britain's top marathon runner. He was a client of mine at one time, and he used to run and train every day. Apart from his natural ability, one of his claims to fame was that he ran every day of his life! One day he came to see me, and his leg was in plaster up to the knee. I said, "Morning Ron, have you been out for a run this morning?" and he said, "Yes of course, but I only managed to hobble a mile!"

My veteran athletic career and The Foxtrotters

115 World Veteran Athletic Championships, Christchurch, Jan 1981, 400 metre race, 45–50 age group. 1st place – H. Thomas (Australia); 2nd place – M. Garbisch (Germany); 3rd place – D. Herman (Great Britain)

116 Me running at Cosford Indoor Track in the British Veterans' National Indoor Championships, 1980s

117 Me training in Wilmslow, 1980s

My veteran athletic career and The Foxtrotters

118 Training in Alderley Edge, 1980

I also knew Andy Carter, who was sixth in the 800m in the Olympic Games in Munich in 1972, where 11 members of the Israeli team were shot and killed. Of the athletes I knew, and perhaps the most famous of them was Derek Ibbotson, who held the world record for the mile. Roger Bannister was the first man to do the sub four minute mile, and then three years later, Derek broke that record.

In 1998, I was at the European Veterans Championships in Cesenatico, Italy, which is just north of Rimini and a very pleasant small seaside resort. A general meeting was convened during the week-long games for the purpose, amongst other matters, to elect a new executive committee, and the day also coincided with my birthday! The British Masters Athletics Federation (BMAF) had nominated me to be the new treasurer. There were two other candidates besides me, a man from Finland and one from Russia. We each had five minutes to address the delegates at the meeting (45 countries were represented) and tell them all about ourselves. I had prepared my speech in German with a view to impressing them. But unfortunately it was to no avail. Prior to the elections, a proposal had been passed to the effect that no country could have more than one representative on the executive. GB already had a member on the executive, so when the elections came up on the agenda, my nomination was immediately ruled out and the choice was between the Russian and the Finn. The Finn won.

These meetings were interesting because you were able to meet all sorts of people. I got talking to this

Russian guy and said to him, "You know I really come from Russia," and I explained that I was from Königsberg, now Kaliningrad. I said, "It's famous for amber, the semi-precious stone. It's found on the beach where my grandparents had their holiday home at Rauschen." He told me that the next time he saw me, he would bring me some amber. That was 1998. The next time I saw him was the following year in 1999, when Great Britain hosted the World Veteran Games in Gateshead. I met up with him in Newcastle, and he had brought me some amber. It was only a tiny piece, but he had brought it for me, especially. I have still got it.

1999 was my last international event because my knees were starting to get me in trouble. I am a bit of a bionic man these days! I had my left knee joint replaced in 2002, which was planned, but my right knee replacement was more of an emergency, in May 2007.

Then, in November 2008, I had to have a new shoulder joint. I had either dislocated it or torn something playing on the Maccabiah squash team back in 1993. I had the operation but then, the next day, I woke up and there was something wrong with my sight. I had lost 60 percent of my peripheral vision on the left side. I saw a neurologist who said that I had probably had a stroke and if my vision didn't come back in six months, I was stuck with it for life. That is when I had to stop driving, and I haven't driven since. I do miss it, for the convenience, but it could have been much worse. I'm still here and Pat drives.

Chapter 27

Our children's career paths, grandchildren and great grandchildren

Linda attended Manchester High School in 1975 and quite early on started to show her talent as a swimmer. She swam for the school and joined the Sale Swimming Club. After that, she swam for the city of Manchester and was selected for the 1977 Maccabiah Games. I was very proud of her. That year, I had the honour of carrying the flag for the British team at the opening ceremony, which Linda loved.

When Linda left Manchester High, she completed a foundation course at Manchester Art School and then went on to Goldsmith's College in London, where she studied embroidery/ textiles, which included religious embroidery. She graduated in 1985 and then started her own business called Satin Stitch. She made *Torah* covers and *tallit* and *tefillin* bags, as well as banners for Masonic lodges and churches.

Linda met Barry Price in the early 1980s; they were introduced by Keith, who knew Barry through football.

Barry was from Belfast. They got engaged in 1985 and married at Tatton Hall on 6 July 1986. Barry fits into the family very well, although the only problem with him is that he supports Manchester United!

We took the *chuppah*, which Linda had designed and made from Pat's wedding dress, from Sale Shul to Tatton. We put it up on the lawn at Tatton Hall. Just as the ceremony started the sun came out, which was fantastic. Karen and Julie were bridesmaids, together with Barry's sisters, Gillian and Jane. My father had already passed away, but my mother was there, and she loved it because she didn't have any guests at her own wedding. The dress is now exhibited at the Manchester Jewish Museum.

Linda and Barry bought a house on Clarence Road in Hale. After two years, in September 1988, their daughter Rachel arrived and then in November 1989, they had Robyn. Later, they moved to a three storey Victorian house in Sale. It was originally my parents' investment property on Northenden Road, which they bought in 1968 and consisted of six flats over two buildings. My parents converted the downstairs into one big flat for Linda and Barry, which was bigger than their previous house in Hale. At some stage, Karen and Keith both lived in separate flats in the same building.

After the kids were born, Linda qualified as a swimming teacher and began teaching at Manchester High and then at the David Lloyd Club. She evenually set up her own swim school and together with Barry's help, they quickly expanded and sold it in 2016.

119 Our granddaughters Robyn (8) and Rachel (9), with Everett Hosack (95) at the first ever European Veteran Indoor Track and Field Championships in Birmingham, 1997

Rachel went on to become head girl at King David High School. Then, whilst on holiday in Israel, she met Yacov who was a medical student. Rachel had become religious by then, and they decided to get married in October 2007 in Jerusalem. She was 19 at the time. Yacov gave up his medical studies to go to *yeshiva*, and he became a teaching rabbi. They now live in a religious community in Jerusalem. They have four children: Akiva, Gavriel, Rivka and Eliyahu, known as Eli. We try and go at least once a year to see them, but it's getting more difficult now particularly after the impact of the COVID-19 pandemic. We went in August 2019 for Eli's *bris*. The great-grandchildren are bilingual, and we speak to them regularly on Facetime and WhatsApp. The eldest, Akiva, is quite a business entrepreneur. He has got a knitting machine in his bedroom from where he manufactures scarves for the family, just like my father who also had a knitting factory!

Robyn was a great dancer, and she went to Cadmans Dance Centre in Sale. Of course, Linda made her outfits. They were lovely, glittery dresses. I remember one day Robyn said, "Grandma Pat, I need some special shoes for Latin." Pat said, "Why do you need special shoes for Latin? Latin is a language," and she replied, "Not Latin, Latin. Latin dancing!" We have seen Robyn dance internationally. And my mother saw her when she first started, at about seven years old. Robyn went on to study law at Nottingham University, where she founded the university dance club. After she qualified, she didn't want to practice law, so she went into event management. She married Josh Lee in 2017 and they now live in Hale, with their baby daughter Marnie, born in October 2021.

Karen also went to Manchester High School and still is very sporty. She was a very good sprinter and was also a netball and volleyball player. Karen made the Maccabiah team in 1981 for athletics. We went to Israel to support her. That was the first time Karen competed in the Maccabiah. Later, in 1993 and 1997, Karen played in the netball team. In 1993, the team finished in bronze position. Then in 1997, the same team won the gold medal, which was fantastic!

1997 was also the year the Ramat Gan bridge collapsed. It was the first year I wasn't part of the games as an official or a competitor. I went purely to support Karen and also Keith, who was on the five-a-side Futsal team. We went to the opening ceremony and were waiting for the competitors to come in and walk around the stadium. The competitors were all assembled in a large field outside, separated from the stadium by the River Yarkon. A bridge had been built over it especially for the games, and the teams were marching over in alphabetical order. It collapsed as the Australians were coming in. The water wasn't very deep, but it was dirty and contaminated with all sorts of toxic chemicals and that's what did the damage. Tragically, one of the Australians died in the collapse and three died from poisoning sometime later. It was really terrible.

The British team, with Karen and Keith, was waiting just behind the Australian team to march in. We were in our seats when we heard people on their phones talking about a problem with the bridge, and then there was an announcement. It was very worrying, as we didn't know then what had happened, and they wouldn't let us out of the stadium. Karen and Keith were very upset, but they carried on. The ceremony continued on a much more muted basis.

Karen went on to study at Alsager, which is now part of Manchester Metropolitan University where she qualified with a BEd Hons degree. Her first job was in Dagenham, East London. She also went to teach in Spain for two years, where she shared a flat with Julie who was doing a year abroad as part of her Spanish and business studies degree at Leeds University. Karen got married on 27 July 2000 to Robert Wright, but she wanted to retain the name Herman, so she's Karen Herman Wright. Robert was a firefighter at the time, but he has since retired. Karen took up a teaching post at Fielden Park College in Manchester, and then she moved to Ridge Danyers in Cheadle. She retired from teaching and in 2017, she took up a second career in storytelling photography. She was accepted as a volunteer at Childline (NSPCC) in 2015 and is now a fully fledged counsellor there.

Keith went to Altrincham Prep and from there to William Hulme Grammar School. He wasn't interested in going to university, though he did once play lacrosse for Sheffield University! One Saturday, William Hulme were playing Sheffield University in a match and Sheffield were one short. Keith just happened to be at school that morning and was asked to make up the Sheffield team.

Keith wanted to become a travel agent, and he got an interview with Sidney Frieslander. He didn't have anything to wear, so he wore one of my suits, which must have been lucky because he got the job! He stayed with them for four or five years, passed exams and moved on to work for STA Travel on Deansgate. Then, while he was still quite young, he started his own agency in Holmes Chapel. After a while, he wanted a break from travel, so he set up a business in the 1980s with a friend selling up and over garage doors. I ended up with an up-and-over garage door! Eventually, he went back to travel and is currently CEO of Trending Travel.

Keith had three children with his first wife, Lesley, called Jessica, Max and Eddy. Jessica, who was born in 1991, went to North Cheshire Jewish Primary School (NCJPS) and then to King David High School. She did an art foundation course at Central Saint Martins in London, which is very well regarded, and was offered a place to do a degree there, but she didn't like London. She came back to Manchester, worked in a furniture store in Cheadle Hulme and then got a job in Batley, Yorkshire, at Red Brick Mill. She has her own office and operates as a very successful independent interior designer. She lives in Leeds and is now engaged to Liam, an independent financial advisor. They are hoping to get married in 2022, probably in August.

Max was born in 1993 and also started off at NCJPS but then he went on to Altrincham Prep and King David High School, before going to Manchester Grammar School (MGS) for the sixth form. From MGS, he went to Nottingham University where he attained a

Our children's career paths, grandchildren and great grandchildren

law degree, but the legal profession didn't appeal to him. Eventually he moved to managing commercial mortgages and loans. He's now settled in London.

Two years after Max came Eddy. He also went to NCJPS and then MGS. He chose Durham University, where he did a four-year masters degree in electronic engineering. He is a whizz kid at computers and all things digital.

When Eddy was 18, he was goalkeeper on the GB under-18 Futsal team at the 2013 Maccabiah Games at the Wingate Centre, near Netanya. We went to support him, and Eddy was voted player of the tournament. Whilst in Israel, we took the opportunity to visit our oldest granddaughter Rachel and her family in Jerusalem. Rachel also came with us to support Eddy in the Futsal tournament.

After Keith and Lesley split up, Keith met the lovely Sara and they married in 2006 and moved to Hale. Soon after, Jack was born at Wythenshawe Hospital, where he set a record for being the third heaviest baby ever born there at 14.8 pounds! He was born on 11 May 2007. Sadly, my mother had died four days earlier. That was a difficult time for everyone as, at the same time, I was having my second knee replacement, so I was in a wheelchair for a few weeks. Jack is in his third year at MGS now.

George Valentine was born on Valentine's Day 2012, and he is a completely different character from Jack. Jack is very cool, calm and collected whereas George is extrovert and a great performer. George is currently at North Cheshire Primary School.

Our fourth child, Julie Vanessa, went to Manchester High Prep and to the main school. She then went to Leeds University where she completed her degree in Spanish and business studies, followed by a gap year travelling with her friend Vanessa. When she finished travelling, she got a job in an insurance business and then at an events company in Bourne End, near Henley-on-Thames. By then she had met Damian, who was from Nottingham, and he was working for a big catering firm in London. They got married in 1997, lived in a flat in Willesden Green and had their boys. Freddie was born in 1998 and Noah in 2000.

Damian was offered a job with British Airways as catering manager for all their long haul international flights out of Manchester. Julie was then engaged by an events company based in Sale, so in 2001, they moved to Manchester. It was great to have the family living close by once again. I had always told my children that the streets of London are not all paved with gold! They had been able to sell their three bedroom 'cupboard' in Willesden Green and purchase a five bedroom house in Sale.

Freddie attended a nursery, which was conveniently situated around the corner from their home in Sale. He then attended NCJPS, passed his 11 plus and went to Altrincham Grammar for Boys. From there, he went to university in Leeds where he studied music production. After a short spell of teaching music to primary school children in Leeds, he is now well established as a music producer with a company, also in Leeds.

Our children's career paths, grandchildren and great grandchildren

Noah followed in his brother's footsteps to North Cheshire Jewish Primary School, and then he went to Manchester Grammar School. He showed a keen interest in amateur dramatics and has taken part in many of the Junior Stage 80 and school productions. He's currently studying a BA joint honours degree in Spanish and history at Durham University.

Not long after moving to Sale, Julie, together with a colleague set up their own events company which they called 'Fresh'. Damian joined them as a director, and they moved into substantial new premises in Cheadle. Together they were able to develop a very successful business. They sold the business in 2015, and then Julie concentrated her efforts on being assistant project manager on a family building project.

We loved our first house on The Avenue in Sale, and all the children were brought up there but after 27 years, in 1987, we decided we wanted a bit of a change. By then, Linda had been married from the house in 1986, Karen was already working away, Keith lived at home and Julie was still at school. We eventually bought a house in Bowdon and we moved in on 31 July 1987. The house dated back to about 1927 and was quite substantial. In 1995, we decided to add a garden room, which made quite a difference, as that is where we spent most of our time.

In 2014, it was the time for us to downsize, as all the kids were married. We looked at various properties, and we put the house on the market. However, Julie and Damian decided they wanted to buy it, knock it down and rebuild on the same site with apartments - one for us, a section for them and a section for Steph and Barry, Damian's parents. While the new building was under construction, we rented a house in Hale Barns, for 18 months. We moved back on 16 November 2016, and we are very happy here. It has worked out really well.

In the meantime, Damian, whose dream it had always been to own a deli/ coffee bar, found the very thing in Altrincham. It was a coffee bar called Common Ground and available to buy as a going concern. He bought it in August 2018, and he and Julie ran it very successfully for three years, despite the intervention of COVID-19. They were able to sell the business in August 2021. Julie now keeps herself busy with interests in two companies, and she is also an active trustee of The Fed. Whenever I ask Damian about his future plans, he describes himself as a 'gentleman of leisure on a sabbatical'.

120 My 85th birthday celebrations in Harrogate, September 2020
All four children with spouses and some grandchildren
L-R: Karen, Robert, Julie, Freddie, Damian, Me, Noah, Pat, Sara, George, Max, Jack, Eddy, Keith, Jessica, Linda, Barry, Robyn and Josh

121 Linda and Barry's 30th wedding anniversary in Dunham Park, 6 July 2016
Back row (L-R): Freddie, Damian, Julie, Jack, Robyn, Josh, Karen, Robert, Linda, Barry, Gillian, Ivor, Yacov, Rivka, Rachel, Keith, Sara, Jessica
Front row (L-R): Noah, Danny, Pat, Akiva, George, Eddy, Jack, Gavriel

© Rob Clayton Photography. All rights reserved.

122 Pat's 80th birthday party at Dunham Golf Club with friends from Manchester High School and our girls
Back Row (L-R): Kerrith Harris, Barbara Goodman, Jackie Mesrie, Linda Price, Valerie Harris, Julie Besbrode, Bette Braka, Charmian Frieze, Debby Carr, Karen Herman Wright
Front row (L-R): Frankie Solomons, Sylvia Farley, Pat, Valerie Hanson, Judith Brettler

Chapter 28

Our holidays

When the kids were young, we sometimes holidayed in Abersoch. We had friends who had a place on The Warren and we rented their chalet. We enjoyed a couple of very good beach holidays there.

My mother used to holiday-sit the kids, allowing us to go off without them on a regular basis. Babysitting was one of my mother's biggest pleasures. I think this made her recall my childhood and all the holidays that she had missed with me, up to when we left Germany in 1939 when I was nearly four. During this time, the political situation had rapidly deteriorated in Germany, and we were deprived of our freedom and choices. Following the success of our first holiday without Linda in 1963, we never refused both *Oma* and *Opa's* offers because we understood how much pleasure it gave them and us! Our friends were very envious of the situation.

In 1968, we went to Knoll House near Swanage in Dorset, right on the beach. We took Linda and Karen, and they both managed to contract mumps! They didn't actually feel ill, but we had to isolate them. One

Our holidays

day, we went out for the morning, and we left them in the bedroom together. When we came back, all the sheets and parts of the walls had been covered with felt tip pens! I don't know how we managed to sort that out with the hotel! In those days, it was natural to leave your children in a room, but you wouldn't dream of doing that today.

The first barge holiday we had as a family was in 1975, a very hot summer. We went from Bunbury to Llangollen and back, which took about a week. However, we couldn't complete the full journey because there was a drought and the canal was gradually drying up. The highlight of the trip was when Keith fell into the canal, and I jumped in after him. Fortunately, no one was injured, but I had to dry out all the money that was in my wallet on the washing line!

We enjoyed that holiday so much that we repeated it in 1980, though by then Linda and Karen thought they were too old to join us. We took Keith's cousin, Kenny Wax, with us and our very good friends, Chris and Jack Abadi, and their niece and nephew. One of the highlights of this voyage was when Julie fell into the canal! Chris and Pat became fed up with cooking every evening, so one day Jack and I were designated dinner duties. We outwitted them though as we moored up close to a fish and chip shop and bought supper for everyone!

In January 1981, we went away for a month, the main purpose being to compete in the World Veteran Games in Christchurch, New Zealand. In the first part of the trip, we flew from London, via Bombay, Kuala

Lumpur, Perth and then to Sydney, finally arriving in Auckland. It took us 30 hours. We stayed with Pat's old college friend for three or four days and then went down to Christchurch for the Games, where we stayed in a hall of residence, student accommodation, with a bed in each corner of the room. The washing facilities were communal, so I had to stand guard by the shower when Pat was in there!

After the Games, we flew to Sydney and met our friend from Manchester, Gita Koenig, who was the lady I bought the cigarette business from. Then we spent five days in Bali, a few days in Hong Kong and then on to Bangkok for our final port of call, where we ran in to my parents' next door neighbours from Northenden! It's a small world! We didn't know they were going to be there. That was an amazing trip.

We bought a small house in Marbella in 1987 and spent a lot of our holidays there. At the millennium, everybody came to the house, and we had to rent a few other houses because our home couldn't accomodate 20 people. Keith didn't join us because he had prearranged a holiday to Belize with Lesley's family. We self-catered a big party at home, and I hired a magician to entertain us. We used to go to Marbella two or three times a year for ten days at a time, but eventually we sold the house in June 2021.

One of our joint favourite holidays was when we went to South Africa in 1993 for a wedding. It was held at the Mount Nelson Hotel on the outskirts of Cape Town, which was a fantastic hotel. I had my hair cut there and Margaret Thatcher, the former UK Prime

Our holidays

Minister, was sitting in the chair next but one to me! I often joke that she asked me for my autograph, as she obviously knew I was the 'fastest Jew in Britain'!

We went along the Garden Route and stayed for five days at Richard Branson's Ulusaba Safari Lodge in the beautiful Sabi Sand Game Reserve, which was magnificent. Richard Branson's private secretary was there and she told us some interesting stories. There were only about 25 people at the lodge, and we all ate together around a big table. We went out every day and saw lions basking in the sunshine beside the dirt track; we were only about three metres away from them. It was also quite scary when we came close to a large herd of elephants. We both agree that they were the best five days of any holiday we've ever had.

When Pat and I went on our travels, we liked looking at rocking horses at antique fairs. In January 1995, Brian Fox, the head of our running group and a great DIY man, told me he'd made a rocking horse, so I went to see it. It must have been about five feet long! I wanted to make one with Pat, and he told me about a firm in Cornwall where I could buy the plans (similar to a dressmaking pattern) for £17. I had to buy the wood and Brian said he would lend me his tools. The horse wasn't made from just one block of wood, but from different layers of timber that you had to cut to size and shape with a jigsaw, plane and other power tools. We then stuck it together using special glue, smoothed and varnished it. When that was finished, we bought all the accoutrements such as the mane, the eyelashes, the saddle etc. The materials cost about £250, but the

123 Holiday in Bali, January 1981

Our holidays

124 Pat, my mother-in-law Fay and me, Marbella, 1991

125 Pat and me in front of the Twin Towers, New York, March 1988

126 Pat's 50th birthday, The Plaza Hotel in New York, 1988

127 Me in Thessaloníki (Thessalonica), 2008

Our holidays

finished article would probably have cost about £1,000 if sold at that time. A friend bet that we wouldn't finish it by Christmas Day 1995, which we managed to win, so he had to take us out for dinner. We've always kept the horse at the bottom of our staircase because if we had given it to one of the kids, we would have had to make three more!

During the COVID-19 pandemic, Pat and I were not able to go away on holiday, but we achieved notoriety by being the first couple over the age of 80 to receive the first two Pfizer jabs in the borough of Trafford.

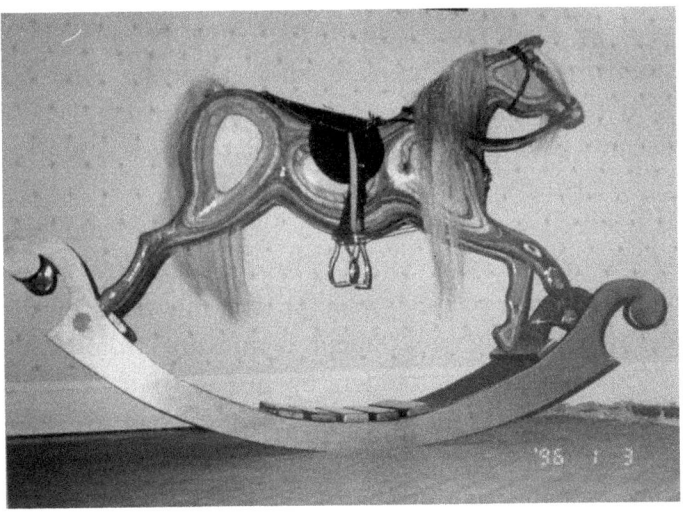

128 'Rocky' the rocking horse, which Pat and I made in 1995

Chapter 29

My volunteering roles

I have had various volunteering roles, some of which were at Manchester High School for Girls. Once when I was watching the Manchester High swimming club, I was persuaded to attend the PTA AGM being held the following week. They were short of people, and the next thing I knew, I was on the committee! Then I became treasurer and secretary. In 2000, I was invited to be a trustee of the bursary fund.

I joined the committee of the Morris Feinmann Home in 1986 and eventually became treasurer, which I did for ten years. I was the administrator of the Barfield House management committee from when the retirement development opened in 1996. I continued in that role up until 2008, when I had to resign because of the loss of my peripheral vision. In March 1997, my mother moved into a lovely two bedroom flat in Barfield House. She was one of the first people to live there, and she really enjoyed it. Her flat overlooked the Morris Feinmann Home, where she was able to join in communal activities, and she used to invite us for Friday night dinner there. She spent her last two or

My volunteering roles

129 Denys Lee Jones, Christine Lee Jones (former headteacher), Pat and me at Manchester High School for Girls Bursary Ball, around 2014

three years actually in the Morris Feinmann Home because she couldn't look after herself. She lived quite happily there until she died when she was just a couple of months short of 97.

I also ran the Robert Whiteson Memorial Fund, which we set up after Pat's sister's son died of Hodgkin's disease in 1989, aged 30. We raised money for research into Hodgkin's disease and allied disorders. We used to have fundraising events run by volunteers. The Valentine's Ball was an annual event, and it was a great success. I also organised the 'Wizard's Terrible Ten', which was a decathlon type event set across ten different hills around Alderley Edge. We had about 30 competitors split over five age groups. The last event we held was in 2008, just before I had my shoulder operation. From that event alone, we must have raised about £50,000. Over the years, we have probably raised about half a million pounds for the charity.

In the past, I have also been involved with many sport-related volunteering roles, including managing the British athletics team at the Maccabiah Games in 1973, 1977 and 1981. I was also the treasurer for the British Masters Athletics Federation from 1994 to 2016.

When I retired from my accountancy practice, I was one of the very first to volunteer for the Commonwealth Games. I applied three years ahead of the games, which were held in Manchester in July 2002. I assumed various roles before and during the games, including organising the flags. Originally, they had been given flags from the previous Kuala Lumpur Games in 1998, but many were not in good condition, so eventually they decided to buy a whole new set of flags. They bought about 3,500 new ones, as they needed them for different venues, both indoors and outdoors, as well as flags for the victory ceremonies.

Both Pat and I were invited to carry the baton on one of the last stages of the Queen's Jubilee Baton Relay, just before it was carried into the arena for the opening ceremony. It must have been one of the first relays ever where a husband and wife handed over the baton to one another, sealed with a kiss! It was a great honour.

After the flag role and before the games started, they asked me to be a tour guide. I took schools and VIP parties around the Velodrome and the Aquatics Centre,

My volunteering roles

130 Pat and me at the baton relay at the Commonwealth Games 2002 (Queen's Jubilee). I took the baton from Pat with a kiss!

which I really enjoyed. During the games, I headed the relations department, and I was in charge of the countries from the Americas, including the Caribbean countries. I dealt with their everyday problems and queries. Karen, my daughter, was also a volunteer and was one of my assistants dealing with the Bahamas contingent. My granddaughters, Rachel and Robyn, chaperoned by my daughter, Linda, were part of a contingent from King David High School involved in the opening ceremony. They held up a huge cloth that carried a picture of the Queen's face and covered the centre of the arena.

My dear wife, Patricia, was also a volunteer at the games. She was given the task of being the private chauffeur to the president of the Tanzanian delegation. In order to carry out her important task, she was given the use of a brand new Rover 75 car. One of her most interesting days was when a Tanzanian won the gold medal in the marathon and she took him, together with the president and other officials, back to the Games village. However, she realised she'd taken a wrong turn and was on the road to Leeds, so she deftly did a U turn and made her way back without a murmur. One of the perks of being a volunteer at the games was that Rover offered a 33 percent discount to anyone interested in purchasing the cars they had used for the games. I took advantage of the offer and bought a Rover for Pat.

After the games had finished, they asked me if I wanted to be a tour guide at the Manchester City stadium because they eventually converted the main stadium into a football pitch, but I decided against it.

In the summertime of 2003, I met Lord Seb Coe when I shared a panel with him at the National Council for Voluntary Organisation's conference held at the

My volunteering roles

Brewers' Hall in London. Pat and I travelled on a first class rail ticket from Manchester, and they put us up at a very 'posh' hotel, The May Fair, not far from The Ritz. They had chosen me to talk for five minutes about my experience as a volunteer at the Commonwealth Games to an audience of 600 people, to support Seb Coe's appeal for 50,000 volunteers.

In 2008, I was asked to take over management of the senior athletics team for the 2009 Maccabiah Games. Unfortunately, I was only able to carry out the role for about a month because I suffered a stroke during an operation on my shoulder and I wasn't able to continue.

131 Lord Seb Coe and me, Brewers' Hall in London, 2003

Chapter 30

Returning to Vienna and Holland

The first time I went to Vienna was in February 1970, when Manchester City was in the final of the European Cup Winners' Cup. I was a bit apprehensive then because of Vienna's history in the Holocaust. Being in Vienna was similar to how I felt about going back to Germany. Since the end of the war, I have always looked at older people and wondered what they did during the war and what I would have done. There were as many Nazis in Austria as there were in Germany, but I try and forget that.

On our trip, Pat and I visited the Jewish Quarter and did lots of sightseeing. We went into a cosy little restaurant where only one other table was taken. It turned out to be occupied by Simon Wiesenthal and his family. He was an Austrian Holocaust Survivor and famous Nazi hunter. I spoke to him in German, introduced myself and told him we had heard him speak in Manchester a couple of years earlier and had found his talk very interesting.

In 1995, Pat took me to Vienna for my 60th birthday to the famous New Year's concert, which is world renowned. Everyone wore evening dress, and there was a big Viennese Ball in the Town Hall afterwards, where we were able to go along and dance. It was tremendous!

In 2015, we went to Holland on a river cruise. We had been on one the previous year from Basel, which went through to Cologne. This one started in Amsterdam, went all the way around Holland and came back to Amsterdam. We decided to stay on for three or four days to try to find where my grandparents and aunt and uncle had lived. We had the address because Linda had taken Rachel and Robyn a few years before and found the place. It was in a smart area and building, but it wasn't a Jewish area any longer. We knocked at the door and there was no reply, so we decided to knock on the neighbour's door. A lady came to the door, and we explained why we were there. She couldn't wait for us to come in and she made tea and coffee for us. She sat at her computer and asked us our family's names so she could search for them. We spent a couple of hours with her, and we got all the details of the family.

It was a very emotional meeting because it turned out her flat was identical to the actual flat my family had lived in next door, as it hadn't been renovated from all those years ago. I imagined that my grandparents, uncle, aunt and cousin must have looked out from the exact same windows and walked down the same steps into the square, when they were taken away to Auschwitz and Sobibór.

Chapter 31

Our famous seder plate

Every *Pesach*, we still use the silver *seder* plate that my mother packed in the container in 1939 in Königsberg, which arrived in England in 1940. I was invited to take it along to an Antiques Roadshow recording by the BBC at Lytham in June 2019. A few months later, the BBC wanted to include my *seder* plate story in a special programme to commemorate the 80th anniversary of the outbreak of the Second World War, which was to be broadcast in September 2019. The programme was recorded at Dover Castle, but as it would have been difficult for me to get there, they edited my earlier interview and inserted it into the special commemorative programme.

The beautiful silver *seder* plate is adorned with the order of the *seder* service in large Hebrew letters and part of Psalm 28 in smaller Hebrew. The plate displays mouldings of various biblical scenes around its outer rim as well as an inscription in German, which translated reads, 'On the silver wedding of Clara and Hugo Herrmann – 17 May 1925'.

Our famous seder plate

On the show, I was interviewed by antiques expert Adam Schoon. I found out later that he chose to be the interviewer, not because he was an expert on *seder* plates or silver, as his field is actually oriental art and pottery, but because he saw that I was born in Königsberg. It turns out that his grandfather was born in Königsberg and possibly his father as well, so we had that in common. He said he wasn't Jewish, but his grandfather was, and it got diluted down the line.

This is what I explained on the programme:

'The seder plate was presented to my paternal grandparents Clara and Hugo Herrmann on the occasion of their silver wedding in 1925. Just before the war broke out, they gave it to my parents. My father was warned that he was going to be taken by the Nazis to a concentration camp if he didn't leave immediately, as the SS were going to come and arrest him the next day. He went to Kitchener camp, sited in Sandwich, Kent, designed to accommodate Jewish refugees from Germany and Austria between the ages of 18 and 45.

My mother was getting very worried that they hadn't sent her passport back with a visa, so she decided that the only way to do anything about it was to go to the British Embassy in Berlin. However, when she got there, an official came out and said "Sorry folks we're closing and we're all going back to England". My mother somehow managed to push to the front, literally put her foot in the door and said, "But you've got my passport, at least give me my passport". And about half an hour later the official came back not only with her passport, but with a visa, so she was delighted of course. We caught more or less the last boat over to England. The seder plate is a symbol of the whole family, of our roots really. Every year when we use it, it makes us think of our departed relatives. You can count them on one hand, those that actually survived."

Antiques expert Adam Schoon was clearly very moved by my story and the story of the plate itself, which he dated to approximately 1910.

Adam said, "This incredible silver antique *Passover seder* dish has an incredible journey behind it. The *seder* dish speaks volumes about your faith and your journey. And to think that you still use it."

132 The silver *seder* plate

Chapter 32
My sporting life reflections

The Maccabi European Games haven't been able to include track and field events recently because there has not been enough support for them. Britain has always been able to raise a team and made a point of doing it, and Israel always sends a team. But now other countries are not sufficiently interested. I think this is how things are in the world as a whole, as we are able to watch both amateur and professional sports more than ever. The top athletes are all full time professionals, and a lot of them get sponsorships. Also, there are definitely two levels in amateur sports. These days, if you want to do well as an athlete, you've got to really be committed and train for many hours, which could be a hindrance to those who want to get to the top. It is a pity that today's youth must choose between playing amateur or professional sports, as it stops people taking part.

I often wonder if had I been a full time athlete, would I have been any better. I think probably not, as I would have worn myself out doing this as well as studying, working and raising a family.

I think I did the best I could, and I got to my best potential, taking into account all the other factors. Facilities these days are much better. The surface of a track and the shoes are much better. Before the 1960s, I used to wear out two or three pairs of shoes a season, but more recently they have lasted me years because the surface is so much better.

133 Me on a training session at Alderley Edge, 2007

Chapter 33
My thoughts on antisemitism and my involvement in Holocaust education

Fortunately, I have had very few experiences of antisemitism. I experienced some 'anti-Germanism' at school in England, whilst we were at war with Germany. I had this instinctive feeling not to reference the fact that I came from Germany. I once got called an antisemitic name by another player whilst playing football for South Manchester in around 1975, but otherwise no significant incidents. I'm afraid antisemitism will never be entirely eradicated.

I have been involved in Holocaust education over the last four years since being introduced to Antony Lishak, a friend of my son-in-law, Barry. Antony founded a charity called Learning from the Righteous some years ago. He started off by conducting a series of workshops for schools, initially in the London area and then in Manchester. The children were aged 14 to 15 and were encouraged to actively participate in workshops covering all aspects of the Holocaust. Antony heard my story and invited me to address some of his Manchester workshops in 2019. He helped me to adapt a talk I had given a few years earlier to the Wilmslow and Alderly Edge Rotary Club, to be more suitable for a younger audience. Holocaust Memorial Day is commemorated globally on 27 January every year. All my talks that year were centred round 27 January and involved talks to Manchester VIPs at the Town Hall and also to all the mayors of the East Cheshire Council at Macclesfield Town Hall.

The last project we did was at a school in East Manchester where the kids heard my talk and were asked to paint afterwards. My stories inspired their pictures. For example, I spoke about having lost my teddy bear which went overboard when I came over on the boat from Hamburg to Harwich. Many of the paintings the children then produced were of a teddy bear wearing a blue and white striped concentration camp uniform. They invited me to have a look at all the artwork and presented me with a framed, A4 sized picture of this teddy bear with a striped pyjama top. There were also quite a few paintings of the Königsberg synagogue, which had been burnt down by the Nazis on *Kristallnacht*, and there is a permanent exhibition in the school now.

JW3 (Jewish Community Centre in London) asked me to give a talk about my life story, similar to the one I give to the schools for the Learning from the Righteous programme, and eventually I agreed to do it on 26 June 2020, whilst we were still in lockdown. I was told 190 devices were logged on and there could have been another 60 viewers on top of that, with people from the same household watching. Apparently, that was a record at the time.

Being involved in Holocaust education is very satisfying because it helps to spread the word, and it is amazing how little is known about it. In fact, my first cousin Edelgard has a son called Frank, who is about the same age as Keith, and he came to visit us in 2017 from Germany. Unbelievably, he told us that his daughter once said to him, "Why did Gretchen and Siegie leave Germany to go to England?" She was referring to my parents. She knew nothing about their story. One hears that the German youth have been taught about the Holocaust, but obviously they missed out somewhere.

Chapter 34

Ellen Rawson

Ellen was my father's first cousin, which made us second cousins. Her father, Hans Herrmann, and my paternal grandfather, Hugo Herrmann, were brothers. Ellen came to England on the Kindertransport when she was about 17. There were 13 years between us. Sadly, she died in September 2019 when she was 97. She was living in the Morris Feinmann Home at the time.

When my father was travelling for work in the early days, he often used to stay four nights in Nottingham, where Ellen lived, and used to devote one night to visiting Ellen and her husband. I don't recall visiting them in Nottingham, and I don't recall them coming to see us. I am in touch with their daughter, Frances, who said that her father in particular didn't want people to know they were Jewish, and she was brought up in a purely secular household. The Holocaust affected people in different ways. However, Ellen was passionate about Holocaust education. She was very involved with the Beth Shalom Holocaust Memorial Centre, just outside Nottingham and assisted them with many of their activities.

These are the words I wrote about her in the eulogy I gave at her funeral:

Ellen was born on 17 January 1922 in Königsberg, East Prussia. The situation with Germany was becoming untenable, so in June 1939, almost exactly 80 years ago to this very day, Ellen's parents had both the courage and the foresight to send her to England via the Kindertransport. She was 17 years old and lived and worked as a domestic with different families throughout the war. When she originally left Germany, she once described how she didn't feel at all sad because she honestly believed her family would meet again. Tragically, this didn't happen, and she never saw her parents and younger brother, Hans, again; all three perished in concentration camps.

After the war, she did catch up with her other brother, Gert, who had made his own way to England. She also renewed an old friendship with Kurt Ratchaminsky, who was quite a bit older than her, which dated back to Königsberg, and they married around 1945. The family name was changed to Rawson, and they moved to Nottingham where Kurt set up a stamp dealership.

After Kurt died in 1961, Ellen took over his business and ran it very successfully for many years until her retirement. She joined the Mechanics Institute, where she learned to be a very accomplished bridge player. Together with her playing partner, Ellen Littman, they won great acclaim and accumulated many trophies. In later years, she passed on her bridge skills as a very proficient teacher of the game, and she retained her membership of the institute. She rose to the rank of chairman and then president.

Another of her passions was her involvement with the Beth Shalom National Holocaust Memorial Centre, just outside Nottingham. Starting in 1995, she used to give lectures there and at other venues mainly to school groups, describing her experiences before and during the Holocaust. She became a very good friend of the Smith family, founders of the Centre, and she was involved in many of their activities. In tribute to Ellen, Marina Smith wrote, 'Eddy and I were amazed to see how energetic Ellen was.'

Ellen's niece, Suzy, describes Ellen as the most caring and intelligent lady. She always made herself available to friends and family or indeed anyone needing assistance, which was greatly appreciated by all concerned.

Two and a half years ago, Ellen moved to Manchester to be near to her dear family. She created quite a dynasty through her daughter Frances, grandchildren - Liz married to Jay, and Will married to Helen, and great grandchildren - Aila, Teddy, Emma, and Ben. I'm so pleased and fortunate to have been able to renew my family connection with her, and even extend it to my children. Ellen was a very good and close friend to my parents, particularly to my mother, and she used to visit regularly when she came up North.

I also read the *Shema* at the end of the eulogy, as a reminder of her time growing up in Königsberg.

Ellen's daughter Frances is a poet. She published a book of poems called 'Visit to the Illuminator' and wrote a poem about her father being a stamp dealer. When Ellen died, Frances gave me some of her photographs, tapes and cassettes about Königsberg. It's a shame I didn't speak more to Ellen because I should have asked her a lot of questions, as she was my link to Königsberg, but I didn't. She would have been able to identify some of the people and places in the photographs. She was 17 when she left, whereas I was not quite 4.

134 Ellen Rawson
©National Holocaust Centre and Museum. All rights reserved.

Chapter 35

We have to remember

Many of these things I have told you are from hearsay, and this is a thread that runs through it all. However, we didn't ask our surviving relatives, and they didn't tell us for some reason, I don't know why. My one regret is that I didn't probe my parents a bit more as to what happened. I should have done that. It is sad and it isn't. I mean, if I knew a lot more about these terrible things that happened, I probably would be having nightmares. My relatives told me there didn't seem much point in going back to Königsberg to see where we lived, or even where my family had businesses, as it has all gone and has been razed to the ground.

My message is that we have to remember the Holocaust. It is too easy to dismiss it as a couple of lines of history in a book. We must not allow the Holocaust to slip away like that. That is why I agreed to tell my story, which in comparison to some stories is quite gentle and peaceful, though quite a few members of my family were lost in concentration camps.

135 a and b Visiting my childhood home at 21 Lingmell Road in Liverpool, 2021

Chaim Herzog once said, "I do not bring forgiveness with me nor forgetfulness. The only ones who can forgive are dead, the living have no right to forget."

136 Pat and me in our garden, June 2021

Chapter 36
My sporting achievements timeline

1945

- Won first ever race at age of nine over 60 yards during street party celebration of VE Day.

1946 – 1953

- Competed for the school athletics and rugby, representing Manchester at athletics and trialist for Manchester Boys at Rugby.

1953 – 1956

- Member of the Manchester University Athletics Club. 100 yards, 220 yards and 220 yards hurdles champion.
- Won Christie Championships in these distances and was awarded full Maroon in 1956.

1956 – 1965

- Competed in sprint events for the Manchester and District LCH winning medals in Lancashire, Cheshire and Northern Counties Championships. Represented these areas in athletic meetings and in the national and intercounty championships.
- Gained an Amateur Athletics Association (AAA) vest.
- Represented Great Britain in Maccabiah Games (1957, 1961, 1965 and 1972). I was captain of the team in 1965 and won gold in 4 x 100m relay in 1961.

1965

- Finished third in the 60 yards in AAA Indoors Championship.
- Gained full international vest representing GB against USA at Wembley.

1967 – 1972

- Assisted Manchester City FC with training with Joe Lancaster and Derek Ibbotson. During this period, they won the FA Cup, the League Cup, the 1st Division Title and the European Cup Winners' Cup.
- Managed the Manchester Athletics Team at Edinburgh Highland Games.

1976

- Started a new career as a veteran athlete (Over 40).

My sporting achievements timeline

1980

- British Champion over 100m in 45-50 age group.

1976 – 2002

- Competed as a veteran sprinter in various five year age groups throughout the period in local, national and international meetings. At the 1981 World Veterans Athletic Championship, won bronze medals in the 100m, 400m and 4 x 100m relay in the 45-49 age group.

2002

- Retired from competitive athletics after an operation for a complete knee joint replacement.

Glossary

Term	Definition
Aufruf	Calling up, referring to the ceremony of calling a prospective groom to the Torah in the synagogue on the sabbath before his wedding
Bar Mitzvah	Jewish coming of age ceremony for boys aged 13
Becher	A special cup used for the purpose of blessing wine on the Sabbath and Jewish festivals
Bris (milah)	Ritual Jewish circumcision for boys at eight days old
Chuppah	Canopy under which a Jewish wedding is conducted
Havdalah	Ceremony that ends the Sabbath and festivals
High Holy Days	Collective name for Jewish New Year and the Day of Atonement, reflecting the seriousness of these days

Glossary

Ketubah	The marriage contract in Jewish law
Kibbutz	Collective farm or settlement founded in Israel
Kristallnacht	The 'Night of Broken Glass'. Occurred on 9-10 November 1938, the Nazis attacked synagogues, Jewish businesses and homes. This was the first large scale act of violence against the Jews.
Moshav	A type of cooperative agricultural settlement in Israel
Oma/Omi	Grandma
Opa/Opi	Grandpa
Pesach	Jewish festival of Passover
Seder(s)	Ritual meal(s) marking the beginning of Passover
Semicha	The ordination of a rabbi within Judaism
Sephardi	Jews or Jewish customs originating from Mediterranean countries
Shabbat	Sabbath. Judaism's day of rest and the holiest day of the week
Schlepp	A tedious journey/ (Lit.) dragging a heavy load
Shema	Main affirmation of Jewish faith, "Hear O Israel, the Lord our G-d the Lord is one" (Deuteronomy 6: 4-9)
Shul	Synagogue
Succah	A temporary structure with a roof of branches, used for eating in on the Jewish festival of Succot

Glossary

Tallis/t — A fringed shawl traditionally worn by Jewish men at prayer

Tefillin — Leather phylacteries worn by males over 13 for midweek morning prayers

Torah — The first five books of the Jewish bible

Yeshiva — Religious seminary for boys aged 16 and over

It takes many dedicated My Voice volunteers to complete a book. All their hours of hard work were recognised when they were awarded the Queen's Award for Voluntary Service in June 2021.

We would like to thank the following volunteers involved in producing Danny Herman's story:

Rochelle Broman	Danielle Jeffries
Andrea Donner	Mandy Leigh
Sharon Eden	Robert Marks
Malcolm Fagelman	Steven Mintz
Daniel Fine	Hannah McConnell
Ruby Gold	Lucian O'Neill
Sharon Inerfield	Stephen Verber
Dalia Kaufman	Robert Weinberg

For more information on the My Voice Project, please visit
https://myvoice.org.uk/

  dictate2us, the UK's leading transcription company, are proud to support the My Voice Project.

About The Fed

At any time, The Fed's services are directly accessed by over 1,800 people of all ages, and 3,600 indirectly. This includes people living in their own homes all over Greater Manchester, or in our care home for older people at Heathlands Village.

The Fed's 350+ social workers, support workers, case workers, nurses, social care workers, coordinators and behind-the-scenes staff, together with over 600 volunteers, provide care, advice and support through a range of projects and departments:

Carers' Support Services
Community Advice and Support Team (CAST)
Day Care
Dementia Care
Drop In Mental Health Services
End-of-life Care
Moorview Supported Independent Living
Mums 'n' Tots Sessions
My Voice Project
Nursing Care
Project Smile Play and Learn Service
The Purple Cafe (Community Cafe)
Residential Care
Volunteer Services
Walk 'n' Talk

Together these make up one fantastic Jewish charity which is not replicated anywhere else in the UK.
www.thefed.org.uk

Caring for our Community